W9-BSI-221

Here's what they're saying about The **Recruiting Process**

"Thanks for including us in the focus group study. We feel as if we have a head start on the new century. We are going to order a copy for every leader in our organization. Hurry and get it printed!"

Jeff and Brenda W.

"People who don't recruit often don't know why. People who do recruit often don't know how. And leaders often wonder how to motivate others to recruit consistently. You have given us the answers and the direction we need."

Susan T.

"When I read 'What Happened To Yesterday,' it made me so mad at myself that I made more appointments in one day than I've ever made in a week."

Rose M.

"You've addressed emotional issues and mental barriers I have never even thought about—at least not consciously. Thank you for also giving us the techniques for dealing with them."

Lois T.

"This is not a one-time read. I'll use it again and again for inspiration and as a source of activities and ideas for recruit training. It's the most helpful book for my business that I've ever read."

Jack H.

"You made me see I've been *looking* at potential recruits and not *seeing* them. Thanks for opening my eyes."

Gail A.

"Easy to read, remember, and apply. We owe you!"

Wendy B.

"What an easy read! What a lot to think about! Why didn't anyone ever tell us this, so recruiting could have been so much easier?"

Marion S.

"It didn't just teach me, it touched me. Thanks so much!"

Norma M.

"I loved Sherle's first book on recruiting and have used it for almost ten years. This new one blows me away! You two have done a terrific job. Let me know the minute it is available, and be sure that you let our home office know about it, too."

Sally K.

We can't tell you how much we feel we've missed the boat. You make things seem so obvious that we just can't believe we overlooked them."

Dallas and Dot S.

"Hurry! Hurry! We need this for our trainers *now*!"

Joe S.

"Just playing a game with myself, I tried hard to think of something about recruiting that you didn't include. You won, I lost. You two have made a real contribution to the industry. Keep up the good work.

Nona P.

"We couldn't believe all the Actionators and meeting material you gave us in one book. We hate planning meetings. You have not only made it a cinch, but now we know how to incorporate something different about recruiting into every meeting in an unusual way."

Mary and Don S.

By Sherle Maguire Adams
and Marlin S. Hershey

PEANUT BUTTER PUBLISHING

Milwaukee • Seattle • Vancouver, B.C. • Portland • Los Angeles

Copyright © 2000 Grandma Sherle, Inc.

All rights reserved.

Cover and Text Design by Georgene Schreiner
Edited by Carolyn Kott Washburne

No part of this publication may be reproduced, or utilized in any form or by any means, electronic or mechanical, including photocopying and recording, or by any information storage and retrieval system, without permission in writing from the authors.

04 03 02 01 00 5 4 3 2 1

ISBN 0-89716-938-7
Library of Congress Catalog Card Number: 00-100145

First Printing February 2000
Printed in the United States of America

Published by Peanut Butter Publishing
Milwaukee, Wisconsin

PEANUT BUTTER PUBLISHING

5630 N. Lake Drive, Milwaukee, WI 53217
414-906-0600 • e-mail: pbpub@execpc.com
Seattle • Vancouver, B.C. • Portland • Los Angeles

Also by
Sherle Maguire Adams

Four Function Approach to Recruiting

Four Function Approach to Training

Four Function Approach to Supervision

Training People to Sell

ESP–The Easy Way to Sell

Know-How for Secretaries

Selling Business Insurance

Run Smart—A Meeting Book

Book of Selling Basics

Planalysis–A Selling Guide

First Aid for Recruiting

Recruiting–The Sharing Process

Thanks to some very special people . . .

To John, my husband, known by everyone we know as "The Saint." I couldn't operate without him. To my son, Todd Lowe, who has been a friend and mentor since he was a very bright, tiny tot. He knows more than I ever will about a lot of things and is CEO of Grandma Sherle, Inc. (GSI). This book was his idea. And to Kathy Richer, the daughter of my heart. She is always there for me.

To Marlin Hershey, my young partner, who is without question one of the smartest, most practical, nicest, and most articulate people I've met in all my years in business. He's making a significant contribution to my life as well as to *The Process Series* for home-based businesses. I'm certain you will benefit from his input.

To Rod Coe and Bob King, who introduced me to a big world of business I never knew existed. It was wonderful to learn that anyone who wants a second income can have one.

I've learned so much by osmosis, through reading and listening to experts in the training, motivation, and self-help fields. I only wish I could give credit where credit is due. I'm grateful to leaders like Neil Offen, who does such an incredible job for the DSA (Direct Selling Association), and to the industry company presidents, leaders, and field people who have shared and taught me so much. That list is very long! I can only hope you all have some sense of who you are and how grateful I am for how you have helped me grow. And thanks for all the great consulting and speaking assignments that have enriched me.

Special thanks go to Susan Pittelman of Peanut Butter Publishing, who cares as much about our books as Marlin and I do. And to Georgene Schreiner who did our design and reads minds. And, of course, to Carolyn Kott Washburne, our editor, who is so sensitive to our objectives and is a delight to work with.

Table of Contents

MEET GRANDMA SHERLE

Some Thoughts from Marlin Hershey

Everyone wants to know why Sherle, who is so active and "young," likes being known as "Grandma Sherle." Sherle claims there are two reasons: one is that "everyone needs a grandma," and the other is her goal to be known as the "Grandma Moses of publishing" in the year 2000. What she brings to the table through her writing and training is truly incredible business experience, an international reputation for "firsts," and an absolute love for helping people grow in careers that bring them joy. She receives standing ovations in her workshops and hundreds of letters monthly from audiences who love her motivating ideas.

I met Sherle when she came to our area as a famous speaker. I was honored to pick her up at the airport and couldn't wait to ask her questions. It was ages before I got the chance because ***she*** asked so many questions about ***me***. This was my first lesson from Sherle: "You learn from everyone, and being curious is a great way to learn."

Sherle has had an exceptionally exciting career in advertising and marketing and has worked with a lot of generals: General Motors, General Food, General Mills, General Electric, and even General Eisenhower. She's known for many product idea "firsts": the first colored refrigerator; the first colored pans; the first purse-sized breath spray; the first game of conversation, Hugh Downs' game Chit Chat; and the first game of optional goals, Careers. And she has produced many award-winning firsts in audio and visual training.

For over thirty years Sherle has been a popular consultant, speaker, and motivational trainer in the growing home-based business industry. This I can assure you: she's a delight to work with, and she's absolutely dedicated to helping you develop the necessary skills to build your future and to help you grow personally as well as financially.

To: YOU
Re: *The* **Recruiting Process**

This book exists thanks to Michael Richer. In 1985 he offered me the financing to write a book to meet the ever-present and growing need for recruiting and motivation ideas. I did it, and it thrilled me that the book was so popular. We went back to press several times, and then, because I was involved with other ventures, I ceased publishing it. But because of so many requests and letters about dog-eared copies, my ongoing interest in helping motivate recruiters, and Marlin Hershey's help and enthusiasm, my son Todd Lowe, CEO of Grandma Sherle Inc. (GSI), decided I should do an update. He's my boss—so I did it—and this is it!

We had one particular challenge. Whether you are with a Party Plan, a Network, a Direct Marketing company, or with any part of the direct sales and service industry, you all have something in common. You offer part- and full-time opportunities. But our challenge was that home-based businesses refer to what they do by different names. You refer to ***recruiting*** or ***enrolling*** or ***sponsoring,*** and it would be awkward to repeat all the terms all the time all through this book.

Because it's a generic term, we decided to use "recruiting," which means everything that is involved in the process of prospecting and interviewing new people. ***So, PLEASE, as you read or talk about the ideas in this book, replace the word "recruiting" with the word you use or, if you prefer, talk about "sharing."***

Thinking about sharing reminds me of how my heart cracks when I see people in the direct sales and service business being honored at annual conventions for what I believe are recruiting result totals that are sometimes only half of what they could be if recruiting were somehow made easier.

Someone once said, "What we can perceive we can achieve," and one of the troubles with recruiting is that the perception of what can be accomplished is often way too low. There are too many people who watch their mentors and see that they do not recruit consistently. And so with no example to inspire them, neither do they.

In the dozen years since I wrote my first recruiting book, I have reinforced my expectations and beliefs, and I have discovered many things. Just to be sure we are on the same track, I would like to share my thinking with you.

I've discovered that it is essential for you to be proud of your company. (If you aren't proud, why not leave?) Your pride is where recruiting begins. A majority of people do not like their job and go to work only because they need a paycheck. What an awful way to live! When belief in your company is apparent, it becomes an intriguer and convincer. Enthusiasm is contagious!

I've discovered that the reasons people *do not* recruit have not changed. These reasons are magnified in today's hectic, analytical society and need to be addressed in practical ways. This book includes easy-to-read QuikBits® that will help you do just that.

I've discovered that the reasons people *do* recruit also have not changed. But today we know more about how to make the recruiting process duplicatable, which is what this book is about.

And as Theresa Soloma, a mission-oriented entrepreneur, says, "If you want to build a strong organization, you will never do anything that cannot be duplicated."

I've discovered that too many people who have great potential for the industry and who would be happy in it are overlooked, or because of false judgments about them, they are often deliberately ignored. One of the reasons for this is that people label one another as too rich, too busy, too lazy, or overqualified. This list goes on and on. Don't label anyone! You might miss an exceptional leader.

I've discovered that you shouldn't give up too easily. If you have a strong hunch, you need to listen to those nagging voices inside you. Whether you call it angels, feelings, or just common sense, these feelings will give you good guidance more frequently than not. As my enthusiastic friend Sheri Lagana taught me, when you meet someone and strongly feel your business can help that person, keep calling every six months or so. You're giving that person a compliment!

On the other hand, if you're talking to people who reject the idea of working with you, even though you know how good it would be for them, don't get frustrated or feel that you failed. They're just not interested now. You did not fail if you were not able to convince them about something they are sure they will never do.

I've discovered that people go recruit-hunting in the forest and can't find any prospective business-building recruits. All the trees could be potential recruits, but only a few trees will end up being good business builders. People building businesses faster than others can usually spot the business-builder trees. While it may take a bit longer to get one, that's where the savvy recruiters concentrate their efforts. They hang out where the business builders do. So can you. Attend their meetings. Go to events.

I've discovered that people often "give up" because they were not able to encourage someone with potential to do what was needed to be successful. You can not accomplish anything unless your new recruits are committed and willing to be trained to get to work right away. So never feel inadequate or like a failure if you did not do the impossible.

I've discovered that people are not like wind-up toys. You cannot motivate them. All you can do is give them ideas, facts, and suggestions to help them motivate themselves. The only way that people will be receptive to what you say is if you are talking to them from their vantage point in terms of their interests.

Most people are insecure and will not be motivated until you have demonstrated in some way that they have something to contribute to their own success. They need to recognize that everyone has some "natural" skills. Anyone who has convinced anyone to do anything—to go somewhere, to buy something, or to eat or try something—is a "convincer" and has the talent to do your business.

I've discovered more than I can ever express from Nona Pione, my favorite mentor. In all the years I've worked in this industry, I have never met or worked with anyone who is brighter, more charming, more dedicated, or more realistic. As far as I am concerned, her judgment is infallible. I hope you find a mentor, in or out of your business, whom you can feel this way about.

I wish you could see Nona doing her card trick. It's a memorable, motivating, visual demonstration of how the law of averages works for you. Nona separates a deck of cards into categories. The aces, kings, and queens are top levels. Jacks, tens, and nines are the next level, the eights, sevens, and sixes could be another level. Fives and fours might be a customer, and threes and twos represent a "No!!" Invariably one person will get mostly potential business builders and the next person will get low card after low card.

The message? We all have the same cards in life's deck of prospects and potential new recruits. We just have to stay in the game until we get a better deal and the right numbers come up. The trick is to never give up and always be patient and persistent.

I've discovered that my friend Tom Pisano is right on target when he says, "You will get a lot further, faster, when you learn the difference between sell and tell." This holds true for recruiting and for the way you present the product or service you represent. Selling puts people off. Don't sell: tell, share, demonstrate, and prove!

I've discovered that you recruit what you look for. There needs to be much more training about how to find and encourage the people who will be serious about wanting to build a business and are willing to invest the time to do it. Myrna and Mark Atha, who work as a team, taught me how easy it is to say, "I've found something we could have fun doing together," and that if you are serious, your friends are likely to be, too.

I've discovered that of all the things we talk about, none is more important than matching the energy of the people you recruit so that you can help them get where they want to go. And as Jim Head, a great trainer, says, "This business is a lot easier to do fast than slow—and going fast is more fun!" Jim always encourages people to recruit out of their comfort zone and to stick with the committed.

I've discovered how important it is to always be a role model and mentor. People will do what you do. And if you don't do something, neither will most of the people you recruit.

Life doesn't deliver a lot of self-starters like my pal Nancy Studer who, day in and day out, gets up and works on the phone, starting at seven, calling steadily until noon and often later.

Or like Mary Sandwick, a field leader who never misses a chance to applaud people for what they've done and refuses to let any problem lower her level of enthusiasm or her self-esteem. Or like Nancy and Henry Noonkester, successful entrepreneurs who put newcomers on a fast track and stay with them to keep them there. Their policy is to match the energy of their business builders.

I've discovered the saying, "The speed of the leader is the speed of the pack," is always true. If you are not working consistently, or if you're not treating your business as a job with regular business hours, meaningful objectives, goals, and plans, how can you expect the people who look to you for guidance to do what you don't? If you aren't setting a good example, how can you mentor and help them?

I've discovered how essential and rewarding it is to be available, like my friend and mentor Alan Pariser, a very young millionaire. All his key people know the best time to reach him. He stays available by pager or by phone. When he can't be available, he says so. His concern for his team is appreciated and pays off.

I've discovered from Bart Breighner's experience as a company president that the most successful companies are those that teach something. No matter what you're selling, showing, or demonstrating, chances are you're teaching customers about something! Make it apparent.

I've discovered how people can seem to be totally out of energy, overworked, exhausted, and too tired to move, and then with just one ring of the phone they are off and running, either to play golf with a friend who needed a fourth, to go on a date with someone they prayed would call, or to rush to an appointment with a prospect.

In all these cases one rule was at work. ***Energy is equal to desire.*** We all find the time and energy to do the things we really want to do. So if you want to be successful in your business, the very first thing to do is to make sure you have a strong "**why.**" If there is not a driving reason or need for you to succeed, you can count on the fact that you won't. Work on developing strong desires. You'll be glad you did.

I've discovered that those who understand the theory of the law of averages have a better time doing business. They know "downers" (like no-shows and "secret" meetings) will end up earning you "uppers." The law of averages takes care of that.

Another wonderful thing I've discovered is how sharing a business can enrich a family circle. I know three sisters, Lois, Renae, and Carol, who are all in the same business, and so are dozens in their large and extended family. The much-increased communication, because of shared interest, is one of the most rewarding things in their lives. Lois joyfully told me, "Our family parties are noisier than ever. Everyone has something to share because now we all have more in common than being related." Steve and Julie Peters, who had a ministry and a meager income, went into a business they could do alongside their work. Today they are wealthy and helping others beyond anything they could ever imagine, and they now have more time to spend with their children.

Every year I rediscover what an emotional business this is. It's more than dollars and cents; it's dollars and sense. Emotional sense. There are always more than a few weepy eyes at the conventions or other affairs where people are being recognized and rewarded for their accomplishments.

The pride that leaders in this business feel is enormous. The feeling of being a part of changing someone's life is incredible. It is among the greatest rewards that the business offers. By itself this should be high motivation toward becoming a leader. All the money is nice, but this feeling of having helped others is a wonderful, life-lasting bonus.

When you come to my workshops or write or call, you are giving me similar rewards. I love hearing how a QuikBit concept gave you new insight, or how what I taught made something you were finding difficult so much easier. Please know that you are enriching my life, just as I know you are enriching the lives of the people you recruit.

I've discovered, more than anything, that we all should count our blessings and walk in joy. I wish the best for you. But do remember, YOU make your own luck.

Sherle Adams

Grandma Sherle Adams

MEET MARLIN

Some Thoughts from Grandma Sherle

The first moment you hear Marlin Hershey speak, you know how very real he is. It comes out of every pore. He is mesmerizing and motivating. He makes the things you thought difficult, easy. That's because he is a simplifier. He has the most structured, retentive, full-of-common-sense mind of anyone I've ever met. And he is fun! I think the reason he has such a good time making money is that, as he says, he knows what to do with the "fear." I asked him to write about that in his memo to you.

The first time I met Marlin, I thought he was too good to be true. When he was still in high school he started a lawn and landscaping business. Before he was out of high school he also had a mulch company. He sold his business to pay for college, where he saw students paying fifteen dollars for T-shirts he knew he could make for five bucks. He and another student started a new business.

While in college he found his love, Maggie, and they now live with the next delight of their lives, their son Sean, in a beautiful home built overlooking water, which was a dream of his.

When I met Marlin, he was twenty-three and earning $250,000 annually. Today, at under thirty, he's earning close to $1,000,000 a year. Marlin's success is based on the fact that he truly cares about happiness, doesn't spend more than he invests, and is always poised for the future.

I've never seen Marlin say "no" to people who are pulling their own weight. He is a helper and a teacher. He is more aware and articulate than anyone I have met at any age or educational level. He never thinks in a rut. His vision soars. He's innovative and practical. There is never a time when I talk to him that I don't learn something. I am proud to have him as a partner, friend, and coauthor.

MEMO From Marlin Hershey

As you look forward to and plan your future, recognize that the need to acknowledge fear is very important. We all feel fear. If we didn't, we wouldn't need to have courage to move forward. It takes courage to reach out and stretch the dimensions of what you do, how you think, and how you build an independent business. What you do and how you handle fear at many levels determines your choices, and choices affect everything you do. If you let the wrong kind of fear dominate you, the chances for success are nil. But there is a good kind of fear.

I've learned from the most successful people in the industry that what makes them operate so well is often fear—the fear that this may be their last opportunity. They know that the difference between success and failure is clear. If you aren't standing on the brim of things open-minded and openhanded, you may miss your opportunity. If your fear is crippling, you may miss that one call, that one individual, that one new resolution, that one chance that by working hard could change your business and your life. So the fear of missing out if you don't tune in and take action is a fear that is justified!

The best way to overcome fear is to face it. Realize that fear is something everyone feels. It can be overcome by action and the realization of how the most successful people handle it. Like everything else in your business, do what can be duplicated, and the way to handle fear the right way is duplicable. Watch your mentors. Consider that the only difference between you and them is that they have "been there, done that," and you're still on your way.

To help you on your way, don't take this book for granted. Use it as the motivating and training tool it is meant to be. QuikBits can work for you in many ways, in a wide variety of situations, and with a wide range of personalities. Do you realize you have participative activities for over sixty five-to-ten-minute meeting segments that you can use to instruct and inspire your people about recruiting?

The degree to which you sincerely care about people is an indicator of the degree of your potential success in your own business. You simply cannot do it alone, or by "using" others, or by not being grateful, or not reaching out to help the people who care about helping others. The fact is that you actually prosper more by entering into relationships of reciprocation so that you both get more than either of you could possibly get separately.

You really need to care about the people you recruit. You have a responsibility to match their energy. And yes, it is foolish to invest time in people who simply talk about what they intend to do but make no effort to do it. Just remember, some will. Some won't. So what? What's next?

Be there for those who walk away, but don't run after them. That is usually a futile effort. Not running after them does not mean *you* don't care, which is something you will want to communicate. It only means *they* don't care enough right now to utilize the fact that you do care and do want to help them. Some will come back.

Caring about recruits and about teaching them to recruit is the only way to enlarge your business. But don't invest time with no potential for payoff. Make it a rule to work with the willing and the coachable. Always be busy adding new recruits to your team. New blood energizes!

The ultimate promise of the kind of work you do is that the work will be personal. What you do helps people find what they want materially, but it also gives them a sense of mission and fun. Your job is to live up to that promise when you can and to understand when you can't.

As someone in contact with prospects and customers, you need to care about these people as well. Cherish all your customers and be grateful for the "repeaters." If you are in party plan, you should treasure your hostesses. And if you don't use hostesses, you should treasure your recruit referers. When it comes to prospective recruits, do not look at them thinking how much money or success they could bring you. Instead, look at them as someone you can help. Show that you truly want to enhance their lives as you help them meet their goals.

Caring about your leads is part of caring about people. As a recruiter you are collecting names (leads) every day. What do you do with them? You show disrespect if you build up hope in someone, even for an instant, and then toss that person's name somewhere and forget to call as promised. Your leads are your Name Inventory. And, like any other inventory, it is what keeps you in business. Have a system for filing and following up on every lead.

Don't forget to take care of yourself, too! I've never known a good recruiter who had an unhappy or worried face. There are successful people who carry emotional and physical burdens, but they keep in focus, stay calm, have faith, and keep going in rough circumstances. If you are stressed and showing it, you are doing something wrong.

Your business gives you something many seek. Most people are more creative then they know. From childhood on people are curious and eager to learn. But for so many work is monotonous and complex, with only a few spurts of productive happiness. This is something you will never say about your work. Consider what the well-known executive Andy Law says: "The power business has over our lives is awesome. It can promote us or dump us. It can offer self-esteem or lack of dignity. It can frighten or coerce us. It can stretch our imaginations. It can destroy families, and it can sponsor and build marriages." Aren't you proud you are doing work that allows more time with families and helps build self-esteem?

It's impossible to grow in this business and not feel better about yourself. And growth is what recruiting is all about.

You can do a lot on your own in whatever business you are in, but chances are you'll never be as rich as you'd like to be. There are only so many hours in each day. You have only so much energy. However, if you leverage your time and have others working, you'll be multiplying the money being earned by, and for, you every hour. That's why you recruit! That's why you never want to stop helping, finding, and developing new people for your organization.

Think about a tiny tot. Maybe you have one or had one. The tot gets up, falls down, probably hurts himself, and gets up again and again. Why does he do this when he knows it will hurt? He does it because his parents are there holding out their hands in case he needs help and saying, "We know you can do it. We did it. You can do it."

That's why this business is more than just a numbers game. Numbers don't make you grow. Your personal "**why**," your drive and commitment, plus the people who support you, are what help you grow. Just as the seeds a farmer plants require sun, you should know what you need to recruit and grow, as well as what inhibits growth. Somewhere in this book we hope you find a QuikBit concept or idea to help you recognize what inhibits you or gets in the way of growth.

Everyone yearns for the sun of a bright future. We all want to be better than we are. We all dare to dream—it doesn't matter what age we are. Think of that when you recruit. We see the twenty-four-to-forty-four-year-old as having the energy, but don't overlook the strong "**whys**" of the forty-four-year-old and up. Some will look at what you are offering them as their last hope and will work harder than you could ever imagine.

Whatever your "why" is, don't lose sight of it. You can win in this business if you want to win and are tenacious, committed, and consistent. You may have to change to succeed, but unless you are willing to give up something that gets in the way of your succeeding, you will never change or grow because you will be controlled by the things you weren't willing to give up—even if only temporarily.

As you look forward to the years ahead, be proud of yourself for the time investment you have made in making your life—and the lives of others—better than you dreamed possible. Know that everything you've done and learned will pay off in so many ways for the rest of your life, in every aspect of your life. Most people cannot say that about their work. Think about what Aristotle said long ago and how it applies to all of us today: "We are what we repeatedly do. Excellence, then, is not an art, but a habit."

So my best advice to you is that as you look forward, you work hard at developing good habits. And every day, in some way, express the love and appreciation of what you do. Our hope, of course, is that one of the things you will learn to love to do is recruiting. More than anything you do, it will reward you.

Marlin S. Hershey

Marlin Hershey

INTRODUCTION

Congratulations on Your Wisdom!

You made a choice. You decided to reach out and do something different with your life. You chose to reduce risk and assure security.

Other than the field of technology, there's probably no business growing faster than your industry. There are good reasons for this, and they all relate to growth: the growing need, the growing skills, the growing potential. Take a minute or so now and think about all the ways that, as you grow, you help people find what they may not even know they are looking for in an industry that is definitely on the grow. And think about some of the reasons why you have every right to be proud of yourself.

➤ **You had the guts to reach out** and find something you can do alongside your regular job (or your life situation) to help you increase your income and utilize your natural skills. You are doing something that will help you all the rest of your life. Every hour you work is an investment in your future.

➤ **You have vision**. You can see a future where you set your own working and relaxing hours, go on mini- or extended vacations on a whim, and give yourself a day off anytime you want one.

➤ **You are a realist**. You know that you get out of YOB* what you put into it. You know success is not handed to you on a silver platter, but it is waiting for you to reach for it.

➤ **You are enriched**. You've discovered that work can be fun and easier when you are in tune with others who believe in the concept of a YOB and have goals similar to yours.

➤ **You are wise**. You've recognized how a YOB like yours offers you the opportunity and value of leveraging your time. Instead of just generating income alone, you have others generating income with and for you.

*NOTE: YOB stands for Your Own Business.

➤ **You are smart**. You can feel secure because you know that, unlike so many others who have to live in fear of downsizing, layoffs, mergers, and unexpected terminations, you have a handy "ace card." You're protected! If you suddenly lose your paycheck, you can always speed up your effort working at your home-based business and increasing your income.

➤ **You are in control**. You are your own boss. When you want a promotion, you know exactly what to do to get it. When you want a raise, you simply work a little harder and give it to yourself. You don't have someone else scheduling your time and deciding *what* you do and *when*. You're in control of your calendar and time decisions. How you spend your time is up to you.

➤ **You are proud**. You know that the work you do recruiting is helping change lives, and you get pleasure out of seeing how you are helping people live up to their best selves.

➤ **You are a good role model**. Children learn from you what schools seldom teach. They learn how important it is to have goals to work toward. While you may not achieve every goal, you are a winner when you do your very best. Adults learn that there are gratifying rewards on many levels for reaching out and starting a home-based business.

➤ **You are lucky**! You have been wise enough to get ahead of the parade and to find the joy and happiness and the time and financial freedom that are only possible with YOB and being an independent entrepreneur.

Pat yourself on the back for a really good decision!

The Process Philosophy

An effective method of doing something involves the ongoing development of all the steps involved on the way to success.

In your company you have a system to follow and a language to describe each step of doing business and every specific process (i.e., recruiting, selling, training). When recruiting, presenting, and training, you want to use company materials and company language. You want anyone you recruit to talk the business and do the business the company way.

You want to set an example that will discourage people from the temptation to do things in their own way and to constantly be trying something new because they are bored with something old.

Regardless of what your company calls the steps in your system, there is a process involved. When you understand the process, it will be easier for you to move ahead. You'll see things as a part of a whole and not get lost or be focused only on what is happening at the moment.

So whatever your business, remember the Process Philosophy. Many people forget this, but ***unless you're actually doing one of the three steps of your business process, you are NOT truly working your business!***

Instead, you're probably shuffling papers, getting buried in detail that is not urgent, talking about what you intend to do, walking away from the phone because of another task you decided to do now, or getting a sudden urge to go somewhere. Do you let these or any distractions rule you because you give in to them? Do you have a habit of stopping work to dream or think about things you know you won't do now but plan to do later? Are you a procrastinator with a tendency to promise yourself that next Monday you will get started? Well, it simply does not work that way. Don't fool yourself!

Do yourself a favor and commit some calendar-specific times to be working on one of the following three steps of the basic process.

STEP ONE:
Exploring, Prospecting, Sharing

This includes anything that has to do with finding, talking to, and developing new prospects, as well as setting a specific date and time for an interview or a presentation about what you offer. The purpose of this process is to arouse curiosity or to help someone see that there is a personal benefit in listening to what you have to say. It is not to give a mini-presentation. If prospects say that they are "not interested," you have more than likely told too much too soon.

STEP TWO:
Enrolling, Presenting, Demonstrating, Interviewing

This involves all the things you do to get ready to tell your story and what you do when you tell it. It means preparing by reviewing a checklist you've developed of what you want to have with you. You should also think about and plan what you intend to do, and say, and ask to obtain a commitment of some kind. Remember that questions are an important part of a presentation because they help you understand your prospect as you begin to build a relationship.

STEP THREE:
Educating, Training, Managing, Mentoring

The educating process begins at the completion of the sign-up, and it never stops! If you are going to succeed, your education must be ongoing. One of the best things about your business is that you'll never be bored. There is always more to learn, more to practice, and more audio and video tapes, books, and other tools to listen to, watch, and read to help improve your skills and attitude.

The best thing of all is that everything you learn and do will help you be a better communicator in all areas of your life.

A PROGRAM WORKS WHEN YOU WORK THE PROGRAM.

If you do not work your company program properly, you cannot expect a new recruit to do any better. Like the process, the program works if you work the program. This means you will be consistently prospecting for new people to help you. It means being businesslike, organized, and a good time manager.

And while there is no need to be perfect, there is a need to try to keep improving and to follow the most basic rule of this business—***never stop recruiting.***

There is a story about a Christmas tree farmer who knew that when he planted four-inch-high seedlings, it would take several years before he could make a profit. Actually, it was five years before the trees were big enough to sell. He was goal-oriented, so year after year he planted new seedlings, took care of them, and prayed for good weather. Then five years later he'd have a nice profit. He did it and got rich.

One year he decided to quit planting seedlings. He took the year off to travel. He came back and started planting trees again. But five years later he was out of business. The year of not planting trees cost him an annual income. He hadn't planted seedlings five years ago when he took the year off, and now he had to pay the price.

Your company has attrition. All companies do. In some it is less than others, but whatever it is, you cannot count on every recruit staying with you forever. If you're not consistently recruiting (planting trees), how are you going to compensate for loss of people and their sales volume in order to keep your business growing?

Never underestimate the importance of consistency. It is an essential part of success. If you aren't consistent, the people you recruit will not recruit or work on a consistent basis. That hurts more than your pocket book. It affects the morale of your team.

Even more important is the fact that if you are not working and recruiting consistently, you are constantly having to gear up to restart your business. What you must do is work at maintaining momentum.

When you set your objectives and define your goals, take into consideration that there are bound to be times you can't or don't want to work. There will always be holidays and, probably, some emergencies. When you can, plan to do more to compensate for these valleys in your activity. And try hard to do something. Maybe you can't recruit someone every week, but there should hardly ever be a time when you can't recruit at least one person a month . . . *if* you are consistent.

Work the process, and the process will work for you!

The Key Reasons People Should Recruit

In any organization there are people who don't and do recruit. Those who do recruit do it because of three basic motivations: intellectual, financial, and psychological

INTELLECTUAL:

Fear is involved here. And logic. More and more people every day are recognizing the dangers of transactional income. It is not steady, stable, or secure. The "be-your-own-boss" and "start-a-home-based-business" appeals are reaching a new and wider audience than any time in history. Time, freedom, and flexibility are getting to be as important as money. Many will give up big money to get a little freedom. Or they will work harder to keep what their money used to be able to buy and have time and flexibility, too. And there is a growing consciousness of the benefits of leveraging time.

FINANCIAL:

The number of two-income families is on the increase. With this comes the stress of too many things left undone at home, too little quality time with the children, and, often, too little extra money. For the average couple the cost of the extra income is fairly high. There are day care or babysitter bills and extra costs for cleaning and other services, clothes, transportation, and eating out. These costs add up and subtract from extra income. It is only natural that people would reach out, look, and listen to some income alternatives such as home-based businesses.

PSYCHOLOGICAL:

Control is a key word. Everyone wants control, but there is no way to have it when you work eight hours or more a day and spend so much time going to and from. Add to this that there is very little recognition or reward for extra effort. People want to be happier, and working a regular job may not be the way to fulfill needs that are every bit as important as money.

These are all valid reasons to recruit, and there are many others.

What if you really need a raise?

With a job, getting a raise is often a decision requiring a "yes" vote from more than one person. When you have your own business, you become the decision-maker. It is like carrying an extra $1,000 in your pocket at all times. In this business you know exactly what you have to do to get $1,000. So when you want a raise, you recruit more and work harder, and you have it—bingo!

Why is it simpler to recruit than it has ever been?

It is easier to recruit these days because the old feeling that a regular paycheck is real security is no longer valid. With all the mergers, acquisitions, layoffs, cutbacks, and terminations, plus steadily increasing interest in temporary help (because of new government rules about fully vested personnel), more and more people want and need to be independent and in control of their own livelihood.

Are people becoming more open to being recruited?

Yes! The demand for quality life is on the increase. Research shows the three key desires today are **freedom, flexibility, and fun**. And *USA Today* and Robert Half surveys show that sixty-eight percent of employed people do not like their jobs. Of those who do, most like the people they work with but do not like the work they do.

How will the growth of the Internet affect recruiting?

Experts predict that while the Internet sales volume is expected to be phenomenal, a high percentage of people still want to see and touch and will go to the store to look at what they are selecting and buy it there. However, shopping at home is more personal and saves time, which is why catalog phone orders and in-home shows are on the grow. Customers like learning more about what they're buying, and they like buying from someone they know and whom they can easily reach if they have questions and complaints. These are the reasons for big growth in the direct sales and service industry. Be glad you're part of it.

How is the changing image of selling affecting recruiting?

The image of selling is changing with a stronger-than-ever emphasis on service. Customers want to talk to people, not machines. They want to talk to people who care. Even shy people are finding that when what you offer has a specific benefit for the user, it is easy to find prospects. People are weary of the time required to drive around to find a parking space and, once inside the store, facing the difficulty of finding a knowledgeable sales person.

What kind of skills are needed to sign up a good recruit?

The wonderful thing about recruiting (or sharing the opportunity) is that you are offering a way to use "natural" skills. Any parent, active committee member, team player, teacher, or anyone who has made a meal come out on time, sold or taught anything to anyone, or organized an activity like a picnic or car pool or bowling league has "natural" skills applicable to personal success in this business. Anyone who has learned about self-management and applied basic business management principles (planning, organizing, motivating, and evaluating) has the experience to be a success.

Why are there so many potential recruits?

The market of potential recruits is enormous. As always there are the successful but discontent professionals and people who need extra income or who want to "job-test" part-time while they are still employed. Mothers are learning how difficult it is to try to do it all. They welcome a way to make extra money or to stay on the career track by working hours that allow them the time they want with their children. The mature market is one of the fastest growing in our society. Healthy, ambitious retirees are looking for work to keep them busy and occupied. There are people everywhere who dislike their jobs or who are bored, broke, or lonely to whom you can offer feelings of achievement, recognition, and financial rewards.

Why are so many new recruits needed in every company?

There is no way to run out of prospects. If you and everyone else in your organization recruited and trained every day of your lives, you would not be able to fill the need for enough people to reach even a fraction of the prospects for the products or services your company offers. There is always room to grow, which is exactly what you and your company want to do.

These are only some of the many reasons you should want to participate in the recruiting process. We would hope that you'd also find considerable delight in being able to share an opportunity and, in the process, very likely change a life. Do keep in mind that we have only barely mentioned your personal rewards. Very much more than extra income is involved.

As you double up having people watch you work, as they observe you, they are being trained. This is a wonderful way to keep you constantly motivated to do better.

As your organization builds, you will learn and get motivated and rewarded by the spirit of others. And because you will always have leaders in training, you will have "helpers" every step of the way.

Your pride in your company, as well as your product and your enthusiasm for your work, will naturally attract people. Your commitment, support, and genuine interest in sharing their success will help retain them, which is what makes recruiting a successful effort.

Yes, there are many benefits to recruiting. If you feel you're not recruiting as effectively and efficiently as you'd like, chances are you'll find answers, ideas, and inspiration as you study the QuikBits on the following pages.

INFOSTRUCTIONS

About QuikBits® and Actionators

Unlike a textbook, this is a book about feelings. It is unique because it tackles emotional issues and mental motivations. It's about how you think, or should think, about recruiting, and it's about what you can do to make it easier for you and the people you recruit.

Your "why" for starting your own business could be to earn $500, $5,000, or $50,000 a month or for other reasons. Whatever your "why," various things that get in the way of your success are similar and "fixable." QuikBits and Actionators will help you "fix" them.

What is a QuikBit?

QuikBits are brief, easy-to-read thoughts that relate to feelings, ideas, information, or instructions to help you do what you do better and easier. Their purpose varies. The main purpose of a QuikBit is to furnish a way to give an individual or group a method for thinking about (and doing some analysis of) something that might be getting in the way of being an effective and consistent recruiter.

Leaders teach good approaches ad infinitum and wonder why someone just doesn't "get it." You can bet there are emotional reasons. We aren't used to talking about emotions, but a reaction to a QuikBit will often give you a clear indication of where the problem is so you can deal with it.

What is an Actionator?

Actionators amplify QuikBits. Reading is not always enough. We all learn by assimilation, and this is never an instantaneous process. So we've given you methods to help make the ideas work for you, whether you're working alone, with your business peers, one-on-one, on the telephone, or participating in a motivational or training meeting.

An Actionator describes an activity to reinforce the lesson inherent in a QuikBit or in a series of QuikBits. It is an easy way to generate one-on-one or group discussions. Actionators are a great way for a leader to plan participative group training segments.

How to maximize the benefits of QuikBits:

Read one QuikBit at a time and then utilize some Actionators to reinforce the QuikBit concept. Doing this will help you get the full emotional impact and the most benefits. Or use QuikBits for personal situations. For example, if you or someone you work with is feeling down or uninspired, try to figure out why. There will probably be a QuikBit that is related to that feeling. Skim through the book and look for help.

If you are using this book with one of your peers, take an hour for you both to work on the phones recruiting. Working as a team always gives one a lift, and competition can be a lot of fun and help you get more done than working alone.

How to maximize the benefits of Actionators:

There are any number of questions, in addition to the ones we have given you, that you can ask about any QuikBit to encourage discussion and a sharing of ideas and challenges. Here are a few thought starters:

- What does this mean to you?
- Did you have any reaction to it?
- Were you reminded of anything?
- Does it make you want something?
- Can you think of anything we could talk about that relates in some way to this QuikBit?
- What kind of activity could we plan for a future meeting or workshop that would reinforce this idea?
- Is there anything in this that we can practice? When shall we share our experiences about what happened when we tried to apply the idea?

Attention Leaders

From experience we know that when you read a QuikBit®, your people will frequently ask you for a copy of the message they have just heard.

Most managers have found that people will sign up a new recruit or two to earn a free copy of a book. Consider using *The RECRUITING PROCESS* as an incentive reward for something you want achieved or by a specific time.

Make it a policy to talk about recruiting concepts at every training and motivational meeting.

Insert a three-to-five-minute QuikBit discussion in every meeting with your group, and when time permits, select an Actionator to use to further develop the concept the QuikBit expresses.

Assign QuikBits to your upcoming leaders and encourage them to create Actionators of their own to generate participative discussions about recruiting.

Also consider using QuikBits and Actionators during your one-on-one or in-person talks, during a check-in phone call, or for remote training motivation.

Keep your copy of *The RECRUITING PROCESS* handy to use. You never know when you'll want to refer to it to help someone or to reinforce a point you need to make.

Do NOT photocopy or e-mail pages from this book without written permission from the authors. You don't want to risk copyright penalties.

1–8

Recruiting

- *Recruiting is helping*
- *Recruiting is growing*
- *Recruiting is sharing*
- *Recruiting is stretching*
- *Recruiting is planning*
- *Some things are easy*
- *To be serious—be serious!*
- *Recruiting is giving*

Quik BIT 1

Recruiting is helping . . .

There are people who are bored, who are lonely, who are broke, who feel unused or unappreciated.

There are people who see no future in their company and can't predict when they will get a raise in pay.

There are people who dream about being their own boss and then have no idea how to make their dream come true. And that's exactly what you can do!

Part time or full time, you can offer a method and hope. And in a very practical way you can help these people begin building their own independent businesses.

You'll show them how to be happy working with their choice of flexible hours so that they can choose what they want to do.

They'll decide how much they want to earn, knowing they can do it with your help and their commitment.

Why in the world would you ever decide not to offer these benefits and deny yourself the joy of helping?

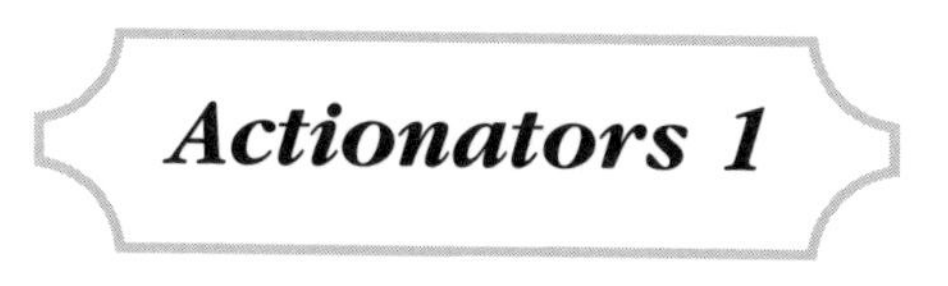

Actionators 1

WRITE

Make a list of the kind of life situations you are glad you are *not* in. Consider people who have financial or emotional problems such as being broke, feeling lonely, or knowing they are not fully utilized or appreciated. CHECK how many situations on your list could be changed by involvement in a career like yours.

SELF-ANALYSIS

Did you find it difficult to make this list? Are you aware of other people enough to sense their problems? Did you hesitate about deciding that your kind of work, new friends, and new activities could be considered a solution? Is it possible that because your life is on a better track than those who are less outgoing, are lonely, or who react poorly to chances for change, you find it hard to relate what you have to offer to their needs? Ask yourself, "why?"

ROLE-PLAY

Pick out someone to pretend to be a widow, a divorcee, a retiree, a need-extra-money executive, a young mother (or father), an empty nester, a newlywed, a teacher with the summer off, or a successful but discontented professional or management person unhappy in a job. Now try to recruit that person. Later, share your feelings as the recruiter and ask the prospect to share his/her feelings, too. Then take time to talk about what you learned and discuss what you as the recruiter might have done differently. Have those who are observing share their ideas.

PEER OR GROUP DISCUSSION

ASK for lists of life situations—job dissatisfaction, an empty nest, being widowed, unemployed, lonely, broke, or successful but discontent—that might create interest in hearing details about the opportunity. DISCUSS what appeals should be used with the particular groups on your list. Have the group talk about innovative ways for meeting potential recruits in these and other types of situations.

Quik BIT 2

Recruiting is growing . . .

Forget about the money or the recognition and the rewards of building your own organization or team.

Just for a moment, forget the tangibles that come your way when you become a successful recruiter.

Think instead of the many personal growth *intangibles*.

Include the blossoming you'll frequently see in the people you bring into the business.

For some reason nature did not intend for anything to grow alone. That's why there are ever-seeding winds.

When you recruit, you grow in your ability to spread the word and understand enough to reach out to help others.

You grow in your ability to encourage, teach, and support as you grow in your skill for mentoring others.

You plant seeds that without your help might have been lost or blown away and wasted.

WRITE

Make a list of the ways that recruiting can help you grow. Consider the financial, intellectual, emotional, and psychological aspects.

Also make a detailed list of how recruiting someone might contribute to his/her growth.

SELF-ANALYSIS

Now check the lists. Put an X after every way that you have grown to the maximum (if you believe that's possible). Then put a check mark next to the ways you'd like to feel you're still growing. If you have no check marks, ask yourself, "why?"

DRAW

You don't have to be an artist to draw this visual. **Start** by drawing a big clay pot. This is your life. **Pretend** the pot is full of soil and seeds. **Draw** a tall stem that extends several inches above the rim of the pot. The stem is your job. Now put a flower at the top of the stem. This is your success. Next draw some leaves. These are your customers, friends, and associates. If you've already recruited people, insert some stems to represent your recruits. And if they've already gotten commitments, add flowers on each. Now draw a dotted-line stem for all the recruits you hope to add. Smile! You are now sharing and planning to share more, and as a result will earn more and get wonderful rewards.

PEER OR GROUP DISCUSSION

Use the clay pot visual as the focus for a discussion on how to nourish growth. **ASK** what you are going to do to assure these stems are rooted **(trained)**? What are you going to do to assure they'll bloom **(get commitments)**? What are you going to do to encourage them to reproduce **(recruit)**? And how do you intend to turn the dotted lines into stems **(the new recruits you need to meet your goals)**?

Quik BIT 3

Recruiting is sharing . . .

Once you recognize the essence of sharing, something you might see as a task or something you *ought* to do more becomes something you *want* to do more.

Take a moment to think about what you are actually doing when you are recruiting.

You share good feelings about your work. You share the fact that your opportunity is open to others.

When you recruit, you offer hope and a way to earn some extra money to those who may love their job but don't like the size of their paycheck.

You offer a way to "job-test" a rewarding new career for the many employed people who hate their jobs but like what they perceive as security.

Recruiting is a logical and wonderful way to teach that real security comes from independence.

It's a wonderful way to help change lives!

Actionators 3

THINK OR TALK ABOUT

How would you define what security means to you? What do you think security means to most people? How secure is the average employee?

How does being a successful independent contractor help contribute to a feeling of security?

What goes through your mind when you can help people to have better feelings about their security?

Can you think of any reasons for not sharing good news about having security as a result of being independent? Does everyone you work with (including your trainer) agree these reasons are valid? If not, why not? It's difficult to justify being selfish.

SELF-ANALYSIS

If you were asked to describe the feelings you have when you do something nice for someone, what would you say?

How would you feel if you had the opportunity to share something helpful and you didn't do it because you were too lazy, busy, or unmotivated?

PEER OR GROUP DISCUSSION

DISCUSS how much sharing goes on in your business and how it affects the success of others, as well as your success.

ASK how the concept of sharing relates to recruiting, and explore what happens if you do it infrequently, occasionally, or consistently.

Quik BIT 4

Recruiting is stretching . . .

If we exercised just enough to not affect our comfort . . .

If we set goals so easy to achieve we hardly had to try . . .

If we never reached out for more than we can see, how would we ever avoid boredom and stagnation?

Wouldn't we become "sleeping settlers" (couch potatoes) instead of being "daring dreamers" (entrepreneurs)?

Recruiting stretches our motivation to reach out.

Recruiting is a method for exercising our willingness to help others stretch their natural skills (and often unrecognized ability) to make their dreams a reality.

It's generally accepted that when you are literally exhausted, exercising will give you renewed energy.

It is the same thing when you get up and exercise your recruiting methods.

We all need to exercise our bodies, our wills, and the desire to grow and help others.

THINK ABOUT OR TALK ABOUT

What do recruiting and exercise have in common? To be a good recruiter, you will need to be dedicated to working to develop certain "muscles." Let's call them by the names Prospecting, Approaching, Convincing, Committing, and Supporting. Which muscle do you need to work on most? Why? What can you do to strengthen that muscle?

WRITE

Having picked a muscle that needs developing, write out an objective and a plan for achieving that objective. Think about this as an exercise program to improve your recruiting strengths.

SELF-ANALYSIS

To exercise regularly takes motivation. What's your motivation for exercising and toning up your recruiting muscles? If you are not highly motivated, can you think of something you really want that recruiting will help you get? And what can you do to get it sooner than you ever imagined? Write your answer so you can see it, share it, and discuss it.

ASK YOURSELF SOME QUESTIONS

Am I in business as a game or for only part-time income, or am I building the foundation for a career with considerable income when and if I need or want it?

PEER OR GROUP MEETING

ASK if any of the recruiting muscles (Prospecting, Approaching, Convincing, Committing, and Supporting) are underdeveloped. If they are underdeveloped, how are you handicapped in terms of results?

DISCUSS what you feel are your weakest and strongest recruiting muscles.

ASSIGN specific "muscle-building" exercises or goals for a set period of time. Schedule a report time.

Quik BIT 5

Recruiting is planning . . .

You're going to find that financial planning is a major aspect of the intellectual part of the recruiting process.

Add to the emotional reasons to recruit the plain, simple fact that you won't make extra money consistently if you don't plan to recruit consistently.

When your recruits are working, you're leveraging time!

When you are a recruiter, you will plan to have people out there doing what you trained them to do and making money for themselves as they make money for you.

That's what planning and leveraging are all about.

When you make whatever you do duplicatable, you will see steadily increasing amounts on your paycheck.

Stick to the company system. Don't waste time trying to "reinvent the wheel."

Get multiple benefits. As you recruit, your paycheck will grow, you will get promoted, and you will learn leadership skills.

You'll be a better communicator in all areas of life!

WRITE

Use the pro/con technique. At the top of a sheet of paper write this question: "Do I want to be an effective recruiter?" Then draw a vertical line down the center of the paper and on one side write the heading "pro" and on the other "con." Now list every single thing you can think of that is positive and negative about recruiting.

SELF-ANALYSIS

Before you do anything else, find a quiet place and go over and over this list. Use this list to try to analyze where your head really is when it comes to giving up things in order to recruit consistently.

THINK OR TALK ABOUT

What might you have to give up in order to find more time to look for and talk to potential recruits? Is it playing tennis with a group? Is it golf? Is it watching a soap opera? Or is it meeting with friends for coffee or to go shopping? Or is it possible that you don't have to give up anything and just have to organize your time better? Think about what you could do if you spent only fifteen to thirty minutes a day making approaches to potential recruits. And what if you rewarded your small children for giving you quiet time to work on the telephone? Ilene Meckley has great ideas for this with her *Phone and Fun* program. Check it out at www.IleneMeckly.com.

PEER OR GROUP DISCUSSION

Compare lists. Do they include "helped someone" versus "denied someone"? Or "willing to hear a 'no'" versus "can't stand hearing 'no'"? What did others have on their list that you missed? Then, as a group, share time-saving and time-stretching ideas about how you can find more time to build your business.

Quik BIT 6

Some things are easy . . .

There are things that we do so regularly we never even think about doing them because they are so easy to do:

Setting the alarm and getting up.

Brushing our teeth and combing our hair.

It's the things we're newly taught to remember (things that are out of our usual pattern, such as recruiting) that we tend to overlook or forget to do.

So it's a good idea to make recruiting a habit.

Don't ever let recruiting become a "sometime" activity.

Make it a habit to be on the lookout for people to recruit! They are out there! Some people are literally "waiting" for you.

Recruit habitually. Recruit consistently. Be aware and always be prepared to meet a prospective customer or business builder. Recruit wherever you meet new people.

The more you do it, the better you'll be at doing it!

Make recruiting you favorite habit.

Actionators 6

WRITE

List some of the things that you do as a habit, meaning that you just *do* them. You don't have to take time out to think consciously, "This is what I am going to do next and this is how I will do it."

SELF-ANALYSIS

How did you develop your everyday habits?

Assume that you really want to develop a special habit. What will you do to make doing something new develop into a habit?

THINK ABOUT OR TALK ABOUT

Let's say you are a leader who is highly motivated to teach your people how to develop the habit of recruiting. What will your strategy be for doing this?

What are some of the things you will tell newcomers to try?

How will you evaluate the success of your efforts?

PEER AND GROUP DISCUSSION

ASK when it comes to things related to recruiting, what do you do habitually (meaning you do it so naturally you never think about having to or wanting to do it)?

What kinds of new recruiting habits would you like to develop?

Do you have any ideas about how to be sure a particular recruiting activity becomes a habit?

Do you know that if you do anything for thirty days in a row, you will have developed a new habit? Have you ever tried this? What happened?

Quik BIT 7

To be serious—be serious!

When you have the gumption to decide on your own that you want your own business, you deserve to be applauded and you deserve support. But if the decision is a whim, you don't deserve support.

When you look for and reach out to potential recruits who could help you leverage your time and increase your income, you are serious about growing your business.

If you're serious about succeeding, reaching out will not be something you do halfheartedly and infrequently.

When you are serious about succeeding, one of the first things to learn is how you can achieve your objectives much more quickly when you recruit so that you are not working alone. Learn how to "partner."

Recruiting skills can easily be improved, but realize that you already have a natural inclination to share all kinds of news and information.

Have you ever told anyone you've found a good butcher or a smart stockbroker? A fun movie? An exciting book? Or that you've heard about a "cure" for something? Or that there is a big sale somewhere?

You know how to share news. Capitalize on it! Recruit!

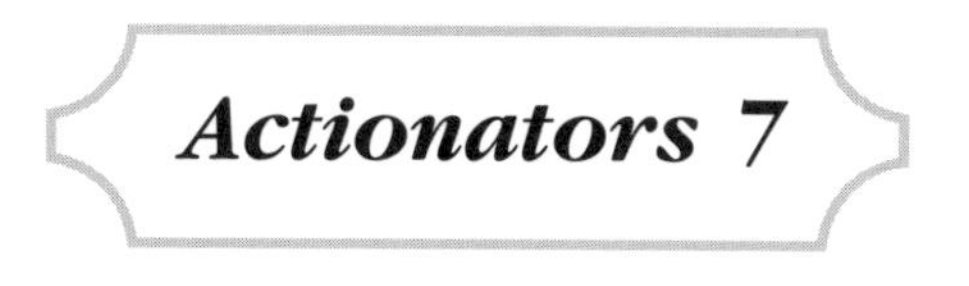

WRITE

Make a list of everything you can think of that you have ever recommended someone do, try, buy, test, see, read, or visit.

SELF-EVALUATION

If your list is long—congratulations! If it is short, ask yourself why you don't do more sharing? Do you trust your judgment? Doesn't it feel good to share good news about something you found that was fun, interesting, or helpful?

ROLE-PLAY

Pair off with someone and think of something you have read, seen, or done that is interesting, fun, exciting, or worthwhile.

Tell the other person about it. Then have him/her do the same to you. Later, talk about your feelings.

Analyze how doing this made you feel, and then talk about how what you did relates to recruiting.

PEER OR GROUP DISCUSSION

Most people like to hear about what other people enjoy. Why is this true? Is it presumptuous or generous to share feelings about something you feel is worthwhile?

Why do you think some people seldom recommend anything?

If you find it difficult to make recommendations, talk about some of the reasons, and think about how to overcome them as a start toward developing the habit of recruiting.

Quik BIT 8

Recruiting is giving . . .

If you sum it all up, recruiting is something very special, because recruiting is “giving.”

It means you give to yourself and to others by giving up something you care about to find the time to recruit.

It means you’re generous and care about helping others find the joy, fulfillment, and rewards that you have.

Recruiting is all the helping, growing, sharing, stretching, and planning that you do because you are serious about building your income.

You recruit because you consider your own business an important aspect of your life.

You recruit because you’re smart and are taking the time and making the effort to build a future.

You recruit because you like the idea of reaching out to help someone.

Good for you!

9-16

Finding Recruits

- *Who do you know?*
- *Think about products and services*
- *A story about a farmer*
- *It's as plain as the nose on your face!*
- *You say you're embarrassed*
- *Be sure to walk through the door*
- *Don't ignore the power of the phone*
- *What you see is what you get*

Quik BIT 9

Who do you know?

Who likes people, is willing to learn, and has done or said something that indicated a desire to grow?

Who do you know who likes, has purchased, or is a prospect for whatever you offer?

Who do you know whose life has changed recently?

Who wants his or her life to change?

Who do you know who is successful and discontented?

Who do you know whom you've never told about all the many advantages of your business?

Who do you know who works for a company that rumor says is going to lay off, merge, or downsize?

If you care enough to reach out and explore the interests, desires, and needs of these worried people, these are the people who could be your new recruits.

It's easier than you think.

All you need to do is arouse their curiosity and suggest you have something good to tell them.

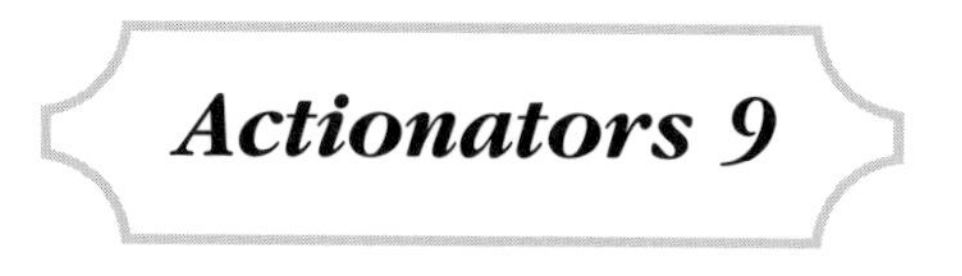

Actionators 9

WRITE

Divide a sheet of paper into eight wide columns with the QuikBit 9 questions as headings. See how many names you can list in answer to each of them. Write your answers in the columns. Make up a similar question for Column 8 and add a list of names. What other questions could you add to these? Write them out and do the same exercise, thinking of names to put under each heading. Think about names. Just names. Don't make judgments about the people.

SELF-ANALYSIS

Do you feel you've thought about these questions so many times that there is no need to rehash them now? Or are you the kind of person who knows you can make the same kind of list many, many times and still discover you've forgotten to include people who should be on it? What kind of a system do you have for recording any name that you happen to think of when you are on the run?

PEER AND GROUP DISCUSSION

PLAY the ABC game. Call out each letter. Then have the group answer with people or places to look for recruits that begin with the letter called. Tell them that you're going to talk fast and that their answers can be silly or sensible. For example, **A** could be aunts or attorneys or apple growers or ant killers. Get as many responses as you can for every letter of the alphabet. Keep the pace fast and enthusiastic. It may get noisy, but they'll get the idea that lead potential is limitless.

At another time do a similar thing with the phone book. Assign the exercise of going through the book to see how many businesses are reminders of someone to call for an appointment.

DISCUSS the best places to look for recruits as well as the many methods presently being used for finding them, such as one-on-one, group meetings, advertising, and referrals. Put the most emphasis on using referral techniques, the least emphasis on advertising.

Quik BIT 10

Think about products and services . . .

Who likes, appreciates, or uses your products and services? Consider all these people as potential recruits.

What you need to do now is be unselfish and share, and be wise enough to study and practice good approaches.

Don't assume an interest in YOB just because there is an interest in the product or service. Interest is simply an open door. It will lead you where you want it to go.

Be sensitive to your audience as you go through the door and move toward a business opportunity. People are bound to be skeptical about abilities and careers.

Focus on how they feel about the decision they made to buy and about the reasons why they said "yes." The "yes" is a reflection of the good feelings about the company.

The potential recruits will then be able to relate their own feelings as to how others might feel, and this will help open their minds to the potential of your business.

To add appeal, talk about your support system, rewards, excitement, recognition, and the joy of achievement.

Actionators 10

WRITE

Make a list of at least five reasons (related only to what and how you sell) why a customer might be a prospective recruit.

SELF-ANALYSIS

How many of your last ten customers did you try to recruit, either by a direct approach or by asking for referrals?

Can you think of any reasonable, logical reason for not offering the career opportunity to every customer at the time of commitment or during a follow-up call? If you showed these reasons to your trainer, can you guess what the reaction would be?

If you can't guess the reaction, are you willing to review your list with your trainer to find out if you agree and if your reasons have any validity? Under the "WRITE" Actionator, did your five reasons include: familiarity, belief in value and/or utility, acceptance of need, respect for your company, and respect for you?

ROLE-PLAY

Take turns describing and role-playing getting an appointment to talk about the business with a customer. After role-playing, analyze and discuss the customer's feelings and probable reactions.

PEER AND GROUP DISCUSSION

Pass out blank sheets of paper. Ask people to write three figures in a vertical line. **First**, the number of customers they have had contact with since the last meeting. **Second**, the number of those customers they tried to recruit. **Third**, how many of these customers were asked for referrals. Discuss the differences in the numbers, and talk about ideas for changing these results.

Quik BIT 11

A story about a farmer . . .

It seems there was a European farmer who dreamed for years about mining diamonds instead of dealing with all the planting and plowing and weather problems.

He saved and saved and denied himself and his family all kinds of pleasures.

Finally, the time came to sell his farm and go to South Africa, where he felt diamonds were waiting to be discovered.

Well, he didn't discover a single diamond.

However, the family who bought his farm found a lot of valuable diamonds right in the farmer's backyard.

When you go off in all directions seeking new recruits, do remember this story.

There are probably good recruits in your own backyard.

Don't overlook the familiar just because it doesn't seem possible that finding new recruits could be so easy.

Actionators 11

THINK ABOUT OR TALK ABOUT

Did you ever have a recruit right under your nose and someone else recruited her/him? If this happened to you, how would you feel? Did you ever go far away from home to find a recruit and then discover one next door or right in the neighborhood?

SELF-EVALUATION

Some people have a "grass-is-greener" complex. Wherever these people are, no matter how lucky they are, they look at the other side of the fence and think things would be better if that's where they were. Do you ever feel like this? Why?

Is feeling like this a way to distract you from having to do something because you've recognized an opportunity? Is it a way for you to avoid responsibility or success? Or do you honestly not realize you've developed a "grass-is-greener" attitude? And if you feel you do have this self-defeating attitude, who will you ask to help you change?

PEER AND GROUP DISCUSSION

ASK why and how the diamond story relates to recruiting. Do you know of any situation that has happened to you or someone else that reminds you of the farmer?

DISCUSS whether a diamond glows, shines, or sparkles as soon as it is discovered. What has to be done to a rough diamond that relates to your responsibility to the new recruits? If you were thinking about recruits as diamonds, how many do you want to find? In what period of time? And where do you intend to do your mining?

What is the easiest or most unusual recruiting example you've ever heard anyone talk about?

Quik BIT 12

It's as plain as the nose on your face!

This phrase is used frequently by a wife when her husband can't find what he is looking at.

Fathers say it to sons who can't find the ball they are looking for or sometimes are even holding.

Every now and then we all tune out to what's around us.

That's why people often hear about someone close to them who has recruited one of their business or social associates, or even a relative or close friend.

Being close often breeds "clue-blindness."

So one of the first places to seek new recruit potential is in a long list of everyone you know. Be sure to list all the people you know and the places that get your business.

Look and listen for clues to help you motivate people to take the time to listen to what you have to say.

And if they aren't interested, be sure to ask for referrals.

Remember that there are "diamonds" in your own backyard. Look for them!

THINK ABOUT OR TALK ABOUT

Have you ever looked for something and then discovered you'd looked right at it several times and didn't see it?

Has this ever happened to you with a potential recruit? Do you think it is possible this has happened to you and you didn't realize it?

SELF-EVALUATION

Even though it sounds dumb to acknowledge that it's possible you sometimes don't see what's in front of you, are you willing to admit it can happen? If you don't want to admit this, why are you so sure you're always aware and tuned in to what's around you?

Have you ever found out that there was someone who would like to have known about the opportunity you offer, and the thought just never occurred to you? Do you know if anyone you know has ever been recruited by someone else? How did you feel when you learned that this happened? Did you make any resolutions? Did you begin to do anything differently?

PEER AND GROUP DISCUSSION

ASK what people close to us we are most likely to overlook as potential recruits. Who do you know who has probably never overlooked a potential recruit? What does s/he do that you don't?

How did you get in the business you're in? Did you recruit yourself, or did someone make an effort to convince you of the career opportunity?

Who has an idea about how we can begin trying to increase our level of awareness so we don't overlook the potential recruits who are right under our noses?

Quik BIT 13

You say you're embarrassed . . .

That's why you tend to never talk about YOB in social situations. You don't want your friends to think you are there to sell them something.

Well, consider this: How do you respond when people ask you what you've been doing lately?

Or ask if you are still at the same job?

Or talk about how well or happy you look?

What do you say when someone wishes he or she could go on a trip and you have just returned from that place?

Or when you bought something extravagant because with your extra YOB money you can afford it?

What do you say when someone expresses a worry, or a wish, or maybe a desire to do something, and you know that what you have to offer might help?

Isn't it okay to say, "You're saying that gives me an idea. I'm going to call you next week!"?

Then you can hold recruiting talk for a future time and go on socializing.

Actionators 13

THINK ABOUT OR TALK ABOUT

How many people do you know socially who are working, but don't like their job or are frustrated or discontent? What percent of the people you know, or may meet socially, might consider joining you *if* they could be open to putting the focus on giving service rather than on their anti-selling feelings?

SELF-ANALYSIS

Assuming you like the people you meet at social, community, or church events, don't you feel that those who might be even a little bit interested are entitled to know about the opportunities offered by your company? If you don't feel that way, don't you think you should do some self-examination and try to discover why?

ROLE-PLAY

Using situations like the QuikBit 13 examples—and making up some others—role-play comments and questions that you might hear in a social situation that could be considered as an opportunity for a curiosity-creating approach.

In your role-playing, observe whether the individuals playing the recruiters avoid letting the conversational "opening" close up without being acknowledged in some way. Discuss some ideas for handling the situations mentioned in the QuikBit.

PEER AND GROUP DISCUSSION

ASK people to share their feelings about recruiting and working with people they know well. What holds them back?

Quik BIT 14

Be sure to walk through the door . . .

If someone is going to "open a door" for you, wouldn't you want to be prepared to walk through it comfortably—especially if you knew it would lead to an opportunity?

Think about the times you've been asked the "door-opening" question, "What do you do for a living?" Were you prepared?

Wouldn't it be smart to prepare a ten-to-thirty-second answer, like a "commercial," developed to make the prospect curious? It could be as simple as, "I show people how to_____," and then you'd add whatever you like best about what you do.

Your response should be concise and intriguing, and it should create curiosity, which is the first step in setting a date so you can talk about your company in more detail.

Or if the situation is inappropriate for recruiting, you can say, "I'm really excited about what I do. I'll call you. We'll have coffee soon so I can tell you about it."

Or answer, and then say something to get the prospect talking, such as, "Tell me about you, Mary." It's that easy to start hearing clues to use as a lead-in to what you want to share.

Actionators 14

THINK OR TALK ABOUT

What situations have you been in recently where there were probably some potential recruits? How often do people ask you what you do or what you've been up to lately? If you don't get the question, what can you do to encourage it? What happens when you ask, "What do you do?" Don't you get asked the same question?

WRITE

Pretend you are a very high-priced copywriter. Your assignment is to write in fifty words or less what it is that you do to earn a second income or as your full-time career—if you are at that stage. Keep in mind that professional copywriters write, rewrite, edit, polish, and write things over and over again, so that the words are as powerful as possible, and there are no wasted or meaningless words.

To make sure that what you wrote sounds like how you talk, read your "commercial" out loud. Talk to yourself as you look in the mirror. Do you sound natural? Can you do it without looking at the written words? Do you feel what you're saying will serve the purpose because most people will be curious? Are you comfortable saying it?

PEER OR GROUP DISCUSSION

Give everyone an assignment to write a "commercial" in the next XX minutes. If you have weekly or monthly meetings, ask attendees to bring their written and practiced "commercial" to the next meeting, and the best ones will win a prize (business materials). Have individuals read "commercials" and have the group talk about their reactions. Then have the attendees vote by applause for the best three.

If the group is small, you may want to do some group role-playing and critiquing. Always have the person who wrote the "commercial" do the critiquing first, then the group. Then the meeting leader could follow with a recap or summation of ideas.

Quik BIT 15

Don't ignore the power of the phone . . .

Some people you know live too far away for you to meet with them and show them exactly what you do, but that certainly doesn't mean they should be neglected.

When used properly, the phone is a powerful, long-distance recruiting tool. You do need to do good service follow-up and strong training, but the phone can save you lots of time.

Make it a rule to work hard practicing "your script" until what you say sounds natural, so it will get results. Then schedule a block of time for some nonstop calling.

Insurance sales research has proven that your phone-selling efficiency usually increases the second and third hour. Momentum helps build the ratio of "yesses."

Making calls and then stopping every now and then to do something else is not what efficient phone marketing is all about.

It's about making call after call with a long list of names, prepared questions, and an outline of what you intend to say, as well as some prepared ideas about how to handle resistance.

Capitalize on phone power. It's a practical way to create good recruiting habits and get new recruits.

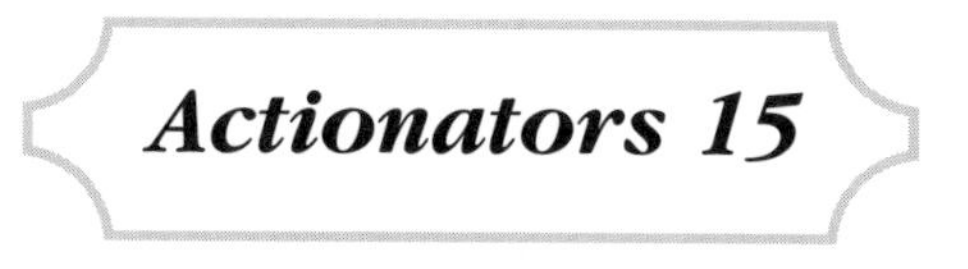

TALK OR THINK ABOUT

Who do you keep in touch with by long distance or e-mail? Who haven't you heard from or talked to in years? Who did you know in school or in the old neighborhood? Do you receive holiday cards from people you hardly ever talk to? Who do you know from a former job in another city? What are they doing these days? Wouldn't you like to know? Wouldn't *they* like to know that you're interested in them?

WRITE

Start a Name Inventory of everyone you can think of who is out of the city. Don't "label." Don't make judgments, just list names. If they aren't interested, they may have referrals. So list any name you can think of. Don't worry if you haven't heard from them in years. Think how pleased you'd be if someone remembered you and was curious about how you are and what you are doing. Now—add more names. And never stop adding to this list. *Never!!*

SELF-ANALYSIS

Is it possible you aren't sure whether they'd remember you or care you called? Are you afraid of seeming pushy? Do you know that when people are genuinely excited, they sound enthusiastic, not pushy? Ask yourself what you have to lose—or gain. What is the worst that can happen? Is doing it worth it? If not, why not?

PEER AND GROUP DISCUSSION

Who has had some experience recruiting over the phone? Does anyone you know have a phone presentation to share? What about phone recruiting experiences? Who would be willing to help you polish up a presentation? What tools does the company furnish to help?

NOTE: Because of the growing use of interactive conference calls for long-distance recruiting, there may be someone you know doing this. If so, check. See what you can learn. You'll want to explore this as an option and see if it works for you.

Quik BIT 16

What you see is what you get . . .

There is a "box" in everyone's head that is filled with one of two things.

We either fill it with zeros, negative feelings, and bits of pessimism, or we fill it with numbers, positive feelings, hopes, dreams, and optimism.

You have to decide what your box is going to be like. It's up to you to determine how your box will influence your life and your recruiting efforts.

Changing the way you see things can change your attitude, ambitions, and awareness and, in the process, change your life.

Do you see potential recruits almost everywhere?

If you don't feel surrounded by potential recruits, is it possible that you are deliberately blinding yourself to opportunity?

17-24

Being Effective

- *Books and tapes won't do it all*
- *Don't scare the new recruits*
- *Zero in when you hear a cue*
- *Is the whole picture too big?*
- *Why some people don't recruit*
- *Two very powerful questions*
- *When is the right time?*
- *It's a privilege to recruit*

Quik BIT 17

Books and tapes won't do it all . . .

There are plenty of lifestyle motivators who tell us to always wear our happy face and "think positive."

We are being brainwashed not to worry and, if we do worry, not to ever let it show.

Plenty of things make us aware that we shouldn't place our worries on someone else's back and that we should just have faith that we can work to make ourselves better.

So the clues you seek are about money worries, boredom, lack of recognition, a dumb job, and the awful feelings of not achieving anything worthwhile.

These clues are seldom going to be paraded before you like ducks in a shooting gallery where practice will make you a better shot.

In recruiting, more than likely, you're dealing with shadows that move and hide in the dark. Clues about feelings and life situations seldom shout for recognition. They're usually hidden.

But with tuned-in empathy you'll often be able to detect feelings and sense problems as you project potential.

Actionators 17

THINK OR TALK ABOUT

What gets in the way of your sensing cues (obvious) or clues (subtle) to indicate a prospect?

WRITE

Make a list of your worst communication faults, things that get in the way of hearing your prospect's whole story and sensing the cues and clues in it. **Here are some thought-starters**: Do you often interrupt because you are overly enthusiastic about making a point? Or because you are certain you know what the person is going to say or ask and you want to save time? Do you listen intensely, or do you halfway tune out because you're planning what to say next?

SELF-MOTIVATION

Promise yourself a reward if, by playing clue-detector, you discover three clues during the next week which, in talking to three potential recruits, were not expressed or obvious.

PEER OR GROUP DISCUSSION

If you knew nothing about the people to whom you are talking except that they know about, and seem to like, your product or service, or want extra money or a new career, what questions would you ask to explore their recruit potential? (Emphasize the purpose of getting cues or clues to use in approaching them later on in the interview, while at the same time not letting your motives be too apparent.)

DISCUSS how to avoid "*topping*" people (a bad American habit) by inserting silence to make certain they've said everything they wanted to say. *Just count 1-2-3* silently before responding.

TALK ABOUT "*structuring*" by telling prospects, "This is what I want to accomplish in the next XX minutes."

DISCUSS "*getting feedback*" by asking open-ended questions that can't be answered with a "yes" or "no."

Quik BIT 18

Don't scare the new recruits . . .

The constant talk about the importance of recruiting can be overwhelming to a newcomer in the business.

In the beginning new people are still unsure about how many prospects are out there.

And even if they sense there are a lot of prospects out there, they don't want to risk losing *their* potential prospects by creating competition.

Ask the doubters if they know the population of their city and surrounding area.

If the existing organization cannot sell and service all these prospects *(it can't)*, you can count on the fact that more recruiting help is needed.

Actually, the more people there are selling and talking about what you offer, the easier it will be to recruit.

It's easier for everyone to do well recruiting if more people know about the good image of your company.

Focus on the fact that you need many more people in the area to reach only a small fraction of the prospects.

WRITE

Pretend someone in a far-away city has said that all the talk about recruiting bothers her. She's a little afraid that if there are too many people working in her area and that there won't be enough customers for everyone. Write a friendly, warm, motivating letter. Put the letter aside for a few days. Then read it as if you were the recipient.

SELF-EVALUATION

As you read the letter, ask yourself if what you wrote would be enough to convince you of customer potential and the big need for new recruits in the area. What could be added? Or asked? Or deleted?

Do you have any doubts about how convinced you are? Are you willing to reveal any doubts that you have to your manager so you will be convinced? Certainly you don't believe you can motivate someone else to recruit consistently if your own belief level is low.

PEER OR GROUP DISCUSSION

ASK why businesses usually grow in direct proportion to the numbers and quality of people who are out there telling others the benefits of what they do.

DISCUSS how recruiting strangers does not have to be learned. It should come from a natural expression of enthusiasm. And talk about how using company materials helps tell the company story.

DO A REVIEW of why recruiting skills can amplify enthusiasm and should always be part of training, role-playing, and practice.

ASK when and how you begin recruit training.

IF you have actual statistics about what a small share of the market your company has, show them as an example of potential prospects.

Quik BIT 19

Zero in when you hear a cue . . .

When you hear anything about a need for money to do or pay for something, to buy something special, or to handle an extra expense—act now!

Get a date to talk soon. Don't file the name away to use later. The situation may change, and you may miss a natural opportunity.

While the need is hot and urgent, fan the flames. Reach out with a solution for the current problem. Demonstrate that helping to solve problems is an essential and satisfying part of your business.

Be specific about discussing the easy steps to learning the business and about time involvement and rewards.

When people have troubles, it may be difficult for them to see help and not feel that they are "dreaming the rescue." What they hear may seem too good to be true.

To be convincing, talk specifically about what can be done. Later, you can relate to their dreams about their tomorrows and how you can help.

Right now, a practical approach is most convincing.

Actionators 19

THINK ABOUT AND TALK ABOUT

Does a cue mean to you that someone has given you an opening to say something? As you read the QuikBit, did any memories about the times you did not pick up on a cue flash through your mind? If they did, try to look back and see if examining the past can teach you anything helpful that you can apply in the future.

SELF-MOTIVATOR

Set a measurable goal to find a specific number of potential recruits to talk with in the next two weeks.

In each case, make up your mind that you're going to offer the opportunity as the answer to fill a definite need. Listen for cues (obvious) and clues (subtle).

PEER OR GROUP DISCUSSION

You are going to hear cues that indicate immediate needs and clues to situations creating needs you could address.

ASK yourself, can you think of any past experiences where cues might have led you to a new recruit? What happened? Looking back, what would you do differently?

What do you think is meant by "dreaming the rescue"? Has this ever happened when you have been talking to someone?

What should you do when something seems too good to be true?

What are the steps in training that a potential recruit should be told in order to build feelings of security about the learning and the ongoing support process?

Quik BIT 20

Is the whole picture too big?

Sometimes the picture you paint for a potential recruit is too big to deal with or imagine.

When you don't know if you're talking to a management candidate, don't jump the gun and promote that person before he or she has even begun.

Spell out what will happen step by step. Make beginning the new career a simple, step-by-step decision.

Use lots of examples (with names) of people who felt like the potential recruit is feeling at the moment. Talk about their life changes and successes.

Don't ask for lifetime decisions. Not yet. Just go for current commitment decisions.

What's an immediate goal to suggest? What needs to be done to achieve this goal?

Talk about "need-to-know" not "nice-to-know," so you will avoid information overload.

Your knowledge is not as important as how much the newcomer to this "picture" can comfortably absorb.

Actionators 20

THINK ABOUT AND TALK ABOUT

Are you a leader? If you are, did you know when you were originally recruited that you would be?

Or did you start part-time to test the waters but were pretty uncertain about your future role in the company?

If you are not a leader yet, do you want to be?

What are you learning and feeling now about recruiting that will probably benefit you when you are helping new recruits?

SELF-EVALUATION

How do you feel about making decisions that involve time, people, money, your career, your working relationships, and the development of new skills—yours and others? Do you think your feelings are common, or is what you feel unique?

What does it usually take to help you make a big decision when you are uncertain about what to do?

WRITE

Make a list of the decisions the potential recruit may be considering. Do you see these as big or little decisions? Why?

PEER OR GROUP DISCUSSION

COMPARE the lists of decisions. Agree which commitments are "little" decisions. On a step-by-step basis, could these help lead you to a firmer commitment from uncertain potential recruits?

DISCUSS some of the "little" things that may have kept previous recruits from making a "yes" decision, and anything that later changed their minds.

Quik BIT 21

Why some people don't recruit . . .

You will often hear nonrecruiters make the excuse that they aren't "comfortable" doing what they have actually been doing all their lives.

So explore what is causing their discomfort in this kind of situation. After all, they have recommended things before, so why not recommend an opportunity?

Is it because they may receive personal benefits they might feel they don't deserve?

Is it because they don't realize the compliment inherent in the selection of someone to whom they are going to offer the opportunity?

Is it selfishness, because their ego is so strong they feel better qualified to do this work?

Or is it that they're simply making an excuse about doing something they don't yet feel they know how to do?

And if you recruited them, what is your excuse for not making them feel more comfortable?

Actionators 21

WRITE

Make a list of every excuse you have ever heard from anyone who is not recruiting or doing an effective or consistent job of recruiting.

ROLE-PLAY

If you aren't a trainer, pretend you are. Take each excuse on the list and team up with someone to role-play how you would handle it. After you're done role-playing, take turns and talk about your feelings or reactions and what you might have said to be more effective.

SELF-EVALUATION

Ask yourself whether some of the responses you gave as the "trainer" surprised you. Why? Do some of the answers make sense to you in terms of your current recruiting behavior and results?

SELF-MOTIVATION

What can you do to motivate yourself to recruit more consistently and to improve and practice recruiting skills? Consider new goals, new reasons, new ways to keep score or compete, or a new and specific recruiting commitment to someone other than yourself. If dealing with small children was one of your excuses, take a look at *Phone and Fun* materials at http://www.Ilenemeckley.com.

PEER AND GROUP DISCUSSION

PLAY the game *Recruiting Excuses.* **One Person** gives a serious or funny excuse. **The second person** answers it. The **third person** scores the answer. The score is based on 0-10, with 10 being really good. Then rotate (or alternate) and repeat the process. Discuss what happened.

ASK who is willing to admit that he or she has been using a particular excuse and is resolved to give it up. What will that person do to help remember not to use the excuse?

Quik BIT 22

Two very powerful questions . . .

When you've talked with someone about an opportunity they're not interested in, ask, "Who else do you know who would ***appreciate*** being ***alerted*** to an ***opportunity*** to . . . ?"

You will get double-takes because of the positive belief that this question reflects. And you'll earn attention because of the three boldface "triggers" (words that will always earn attention).

And you will very likely get some new referral names. Use the question and keep result scores. Discover how well the question works when you use the exact words.

Or try the "Colombo Approach." Seem to accept a "no" and get up to leave. Before going out the door, come back and sit down or stand near the person. Put your materials down, saying, "I have one question I just *have* to ask you. It'll only take a minute."

Quietly, slowly, and sincerely, ask, "If you knew as much as I do about (name of company), and if you felt as strongly as I do that (name of company) would be right for you, what would you have done or said or asked that I didn't?" Then be still and let silence work for you. The answer is always helpful.

Quik BIT 23

When is the right time?

If you're monologing through a recruiting interview, you will not know the time to assume (or get) a commitment.

You have to listen with total empathy, because other than a few obscure body language signals, you won't know what the prospect is feeling.

And unless you realize that you can't hear what a person is *saying* until you know what the person is *feeling*, you won't sense the subtle signals.

Take time to really listen by trying never to interrupt or to "top" what someone is saying.

Tune in with empathy.

Ask open-ended questions to get at the feelings that hide behind words.

Be sensitive to the other person's vantage point, possible doubts, and maybe even fears.

Focus on what the other person is *thinking* instead of on what you know, believe, and want to express.

Quik BIT 24

It's a privilege to recruit . . .

Being effective is not a result of professionalism or learned or practiced skills.

Being an effective recruiter is similar to being a friend, sibling, or parent.

You have a zillion skills that are so natural you never even think about them.

Many of these skills are exactly what will make you a sincere, effective recruiter.

If you care, if you want to help others, if you are willing to reach out, to sometimes get a "no," and to keep on going—you will succeed.

Recruiting is easy if you think of it as something you've been given as a gift to do.

Recruiting is effective when you think of it as a gift you are giving to someone.

Consider yourself among the privileged who are in a position to help others.

25-32

Dealing With People

- *Consider the watermelon*
- *Do you have tunnel vision?*
- *Are they limiting themselves?*
- *When enthusiasm is a disadvantage*
- *Talent may seem unattainable*
- *Are people who they seem to be?*
- *Do you know what motivates me?*
- *Being shy can be an asset*

Actionators for QuikBits 25–33

QuikBits 25-33 are concerned with how to deal with the nagging and unexpressed doubts that many people have about their ability and chances for success in your business. To avoid redundancy, you will not find a separate Actionator for each QuikBit. The activity suggestions on this page will work for all of them.

THINK AND TALK ABOUT

As you read each QuikBit in this section, try to relate it to yourself, to people you tried to recruit or want to recruit, and also to someone in the business whom you really want to help. Can you think of anyone you did not recruit because of what the QuikBit discusses? At that time, did you understand what was going on? What do you intend to do differently so this won't happen again?

List other types of "people-challenges" that you and your peers would like to hear discussed at a future training meeting.

ROLE-PLAY

Take each situation mentioned and turn it into a role-playing session. Be sure to let the role-players critique and comment on what happened first, then discuss their criticism and ideas.

PEER OR GROUP DISCUSSION

Have the group read a QuikBit and decide how to handle the particular situation. **ASK** what is your opinion of the thought expressed in this particular QuikBit? Can you relate it to anything which has happened to you? Have you ever met someone who seemed to fit this behavior description? If you were a leader/trainer and wanted to build a training program around the concept that's expressed in the QuikBit, what would you do before, during, and after the training class?

Quik BIT 25

Consider the watermelon . . .

Think about a delicious watermelon on a hot and humid day, or as a surprising and delicious winter treat.

But consider the problem with watermelon: you have to deal with the seeds. And seeds are a nuisance, aren't they? They get in the way when you're hungry or in a hurry. They slow progress.

But ask yourself this: would you want to give up the delight of eating the watermelon just because of the nuisance of having to deal with the seeds?

Should you give up recruiting because you've found some bad seeds in your organization—people who weren't what they seemed to be?

Remember, recruiting has nothing to do with perfection. Some people aren't what they seem to be.

Some people slow you up and eat up your time. If you don't understand this, you will break your own heart.

Is the effort worth the reward? Should we accept the seeds as part of reality? Yes, we should! Why not?

Quik BIT 26

Do you have tunnel vision?

Is it possible you feel so strongly about your reasons for getting into the business that you have tunnel vision about the motives of others?

If you were a bored executive, unemployed, or a young mother seeing a perfect solution to money problems or to working and being home after school, this does not mean that *your* motivation is the same, the best, or the only motivation for *others*.

They may want money more than you do. Or promotion and recognition. Or trips. Or not being just an employee anymore. Or "getting out" and away from home where most of their time is spent with their children. Or they may like helping people.

If you wanted just a little extra income and then switched to full time when you saw the big picture, this does *not* mean that everyone has the same motivation.

Here's a rule to remember: assumption is the single, biggest cause of communication breakdowns.

So in recruiting, don't assume. Always explore.

Quik BIT 27

Are they limiting themselves?

If people are not recruiting because they fear failure, you are not likely to hear the words, "I'm afraid that I would fail!" They tend to hide their feelings.

Instead, what you hear is, "That's not for me," or, "I could never do that," or, "I'm not interested in recruiting."

You do the person a disservice if you settle simply for what is said. Instead, respond and react to what is really meant. Look for hidden reasons.

If you sense the fear of failure, talk about the flexible support system and how it'll work for and help the person to whom you are talking.

Emphasize the importance of trying—that no matter what happens, there is a payoff. Talk about the benefits of improving communication skills.

Be reassuring.

Generalities are not likely to work as well as asking for a chance to help them reach out and try to recruit someone they think might do well in your business.

Talk about being partners, and then *really* be one!

Quik BIT 28

When enthusiasm is a disadvantage . . .

It is okay to be enthusiastic about the company and the opportunity, but be temperate in your enthusiasm about the chances for someone's success whenever you sense the prospect has any self-doubts.

When people feel you've seen in them things that they are not sure exist, it's possible they may back away because they don't want to disappoint you by being less than you expect.

This is no time for superlatives. It's the time for facts.

Relate "natural" skills or business experience to what you do in a take-for-granted way. That way, the prospect is more likely to understand that there is a chance for success, and you're not just "selling."

No one wants to be sold. When selling is at its very best, it is helping people convince themselves to do something that is good for them.

Know you are on shaky ground. And the only way to get a firm footing is to tell some stories that make prospects think, "That's for me! I want that!" or, "I could do that!" or, "Why don't I give it a try?"

Quik BIT 29

Talent may seem unattainable . . .

When your potential recruit looks at demonstrating, speaking, or selling as something s/he could never do—recognize the communication barrier.

It's true that most recruits may never do these things as well as their favorite, more experienced mentors.

What people fail to see is how practice, exposure, desire, need, intent, and satisfaction can contribute to making them much more skillful than they'd ever imagine. Do you know anyone who has experienced this?

There are many public speakers and famous stars who panic with fear before performances. They're stars, and they stay stars, because they're frightened of not being as good as their audience expects them to be.

That is why they always try harder.

To be successful, realize this: things you thought you could never do, you will do well, simply because you keep trying and practicing.

And most importantly, show them *you care about helping them.* That is where real success begins.

Quik BIT 30

Are people who they seem to be?

People you know who are aggressive, outgoing, and seem so sure of themselves may be filled with more doubts and insecurities than the shyest person you will ever know.

In psychology this is called "reaction formation." And it can fool very wise and discerning people.

So when recruiting outgoing personalities, don't assume you won't have to deal with doubts and fears.

Instead, be sure to build into your recruiting conversations everything you can about the law of averages, the key steps to success, and the opportunities for ongoing support.

These kinds of people need to hear things that will assure them that they won't be thrown in the water until they are certain they can "swim safely."

In recruiting, improve your ability by understanding all the options you have for dealing with a variety of personalities.

Stay flexible. Keep learning. Know that the way people act is not always a true picture of who they are or how they think and feel.

Quik BIT 31

Do you know what motivates me?

If I know you are trying to recruit me, and if something would motivate me to say "yes" to your offer, I may not want you to know what it is.

Even though you may suspect what it is, will I tell you if you're right? Of course not! I will come up with excuses, doubts, and logical-sounding rationalizations.

I will work so hard at not letting you convince me that I'll hardly hear the appealing facts you presented.

The key to the challenge of clue-catching is not what you say to try to flush out the positive responses or the fresh clues. It's what you ask.

You need thoughtful questions that simply can't be answered "yes" or "no." You want feedback. Lots of it!

You want to ask questions that will encourage answers that come from the heart instead of from a hidden reluctance.

You want to sense what I'm feeling behind what I'm saying. You need that knowledge to get a "yes."

Quik BIT 32

Being shy can be an asset . . .

When you are proficient at what you do, potential recruits are likely to think or say, "I could never do that like you do it!" or, "I'm not interested in doing what you do."

You usually recognize shyness, so tune in to the expected before the negative is expressed. But if the negative is expressed, do have a comeback ready to use. Try something like this: "I'm sorry, there is something I should have told you that crossed my mind. It's about why you may be better at this business than I am."

You've aroused curiosity. Bet on it! Go on and explain.

"Because I'm so naturally enthusiastic, when I say 'Hello,' it often sounds like I am selling the day. But some people just don't believe that enthusiasm is real."

"In contrast, you are quieter and more comfortable to listen to, and as a result, you'll have great credibility and are bound to do very well."

After recruiting, warn them not to catch SNIOOP, which stands for the Subtle Negative Influence Of Other People.

33-38

Diluting Negatives

- *Not everyone likes selling*
- *Watch out for the rocks!*
- *What to do instead of sell*
- *Ever worked with a reluctant prospect?*
- *Everyone you know is qualified*
- *Life is about convincing*

Actionators for QuikBits 33–38

QuikBits 33-38 are concerned with how to dilute the negative feelings that some people often have about "selling." Apply these Actionators.

WRITE

Think about yourself and the outstanding people you have met or heard about in the company. Develop a detailed list about what you feel motivates them to talk to prospects, make presentations, perform demonstrations, express benefits, get orders, and obtain referrals.

Now list the ways people who are negative about selling feel about the motives of people who sell. Can you find any of these motives on the first list you prepared? When you do, make a check mark. If your list is complete, there will be a surprising number of motives that will not be checked. What does that tell you?

SELF-ANALYSIS

Knowing that many people have reservations about selling, when someone asks you what you do, how do you answer? Do you say you're in sales (which is not very likely to generate interest, admiration, curiosity, or discussion)? Or do you express excitement about what you do, how you help people, and hint at why what you do is so rewarding?

PEER OR GROUP DISCUSSION

USE a QuikBit to help structure a discussion by explaining that you want to talk about how people feel about salespeople, some of the reasons they feel this way, why these feelings are inappropriate in terms of what you do, and what you could consider doing to alleviate these negative reactions when you are recruiting.

SHARE some experiences about personal contacts with different types of salespeople. Include disappointments and successes.

DISCUSS how to deal with anti-selling attitudes if you feel they exist in someone you want to recruit.

Quik BIT 33

Not everyone likes selling . . .

Believing is like having skin. You don't take beliefs out of the closet of your mind to wear only when it is convenient.

A belief is part of all you are and say and do, and it simply can't be hidden.

Because you believe in the value of what you do and care about your work, your achievements, your new friends, and the way you serve your customers and recruits—your beliefs will show.

The way belief shows is an essential part of why you will successfully recruit new people.

It starts by generating envy of the pride you have in your job in those who feel less lucky. And it usually encourages curiosity about what it is you do for a living.

And, if you're alert, it will help you start a discussion that you can direct toward where you want it to go—to the availability and uniqueness of the opportunity you are privileged to be able to share.

Gradually, as you talk about the service aspects of your business, the negatives about selling will be erased.

Quik BIT 34

Watch out for the rocks!

Of all the rocks on the road to recruiting success, the biggest has to be when people feel negative about the idea of selling or being sold.

Think about this: why don't people say, "I'm going out buying" as often as they say, "I'm going out shopping."

Who would want to be heard admitting, "I like to spend money," instead of, "I'm just going to look around?"

People don't really like to be sold on buying something. So they tend to hesitate about making commitments.

They are often wary about those who are trying to sell them, even if they like the salesperson.

When you recognize this, you'll try harder to put more focus on the benefits and service of what you offer.

Doing this will help you to help people look at you less as a "seller" and more as a "helper."

And that's a very good way to begin a relationship.

It gets rid of a big rock on the road to success.

Quik BIT 35

What to do instead of sell . . .

You'll be more comfortable in any presentation situation when you are telling and not selling.

So get rid of the old sales lingo in your head. It doesn't belong in your vocabulary anymore. Be contemporary!

Focus on helping, not pushing. Telling, not selling.

When you sell, you are under pressure to "close." When you tell, you are explaining something appealing that you want listeners to understand so they will be enthusiastic about wanting to make a "commitment."

You don't have to "handle objections." If your program is right, there's nothing to object to. But it's only natural to have to deal with resistance.

Don't forget, there will probably never be any resistance you shouldn't expect. There are few surprises.

Get rid of expected resistance up front. If you know I'm likely to say, "I'm busy," say, "I want to talk to you. You're the busiest person I know."

Think ahead to get ahead!

Quik BIT 36

Ever worked with a reluctant prospect?

There are people who back away from saying "yes" because they simply can't imagine making money selling to friends and relatives.

They aren't sure where else to find their first prospects.

Change their emphasis!

They're focusing on what *they* stand to gain and feel this will be obvious. That's why they don't want to be seen as a hard-sell salesperson "using" a friend.

What if they knew a better doctor, a better supermarket, a great mechanic, a fabulous movie, or a really exciting book? Would they keep it secret? Ask them.

Wouldn't the same hold true about an easier way to earn money by working flexible hours that fit varying lifestyles and life situations?

What about a way to "job-test" and not have it interfere with a regular job? Isn't that good news?

Shouldn't you feel that people you know and like are entitled to hear good news?

Quik BIT 37

Everyone you know is qualified . . .

What we need to realize is that life prepares all of us to be qualified in many ways to be in sales.

Every time we convince someone about something, like where to go, what to buy, or even to get married, we are ***selling!*** Because "selling" is simply "convincing."

When people react negatively to the idea of selling, they are relating to a past experience with a pushy person who tried unsuccessfully to sell them something.

By contrast, in your business when you're convincing someone about things that have purpose, you're ***helping***, ***serving***, and ***assisting*** people in making a decision you honestly feel is good for them.

Whether you're talking to a top executive, someone who is in middle management, a couple, or a homemaker, all you need is to be natural. Just be you!

People "sell" whenever they ask someone for a decision.

So selling is a natural and much-used skill!

Quik BIT 38

Life is about convincing . . .

From the time we start crying in our cribs to convince our parents that we need attention, we spend much of our lives convincing someone about something.

Convincing skills come naturally. We are all involved in convincing, to one degree or another, every day of our lives—even if it's just talking to ourselves.

Some people are a bit better at convincing than others, but the more we do it, the better we get.

When a woman wants a new couch she doesn't need, or her husband wants to go fishing on their anniversary, convincing skills are needed.

That's one of the bonuses of this business. You learn the methods of being a more effective communicator and a more efficient convincer.

This is a valuable asset in all areas of your life.

How can people let an old-fashioned barrier against selling keep them from practicing a skill like recruiting, which will help them in whatever they do?

39-44

Training and Retention

- *Will your new recruit stay?*
- *What are the first things you did and said?*
- *Don't let excitement take over*
- *People are not sponges*
- *Maintaining recruiting momentum*
- *There's disappointment and joy*

Actionators for QuikBits 39–44

QuikBits 39-44 have to do with how recruiting, training, and retention are related. There is much more to this subject than the few thoughts we've given you to consider here, so we hope you will think about this important subject frequently. Probably no element in recruiting is more critical than recognizing the significance of the recruit's first impression of what you do and how you do it, which in reality is where training the new recruit begins.

How new recruits start training, the enthusiasm they have, and what kind of expectations exist are all determined in part by what you've said and reflected in your approach and presentation to them.

What your new recruit learns in the initial training sessions with you will be in direct proportion to how comfortable the new recruit is in the training situation. Make sure you keep your promises.

Is the training as helpful as you said it would be? Is the trainee excited, enthusiastic, and pleased about getting started? If not, why not? Does the trainee realize that whatever s/he is doing, it is only a first step in the training process? Does the trainee know what to do next? Is s/he committed to doing it?

DISCUSS

How does the Golden Rule apply to the treatment of a new recruit, and why is following this rule so necessary? How will training and the level of enthusiasm affect retention? What are some of the bad things that can happen after a recruit is signed up? What are some of the good things? What about people who might like to recruit but don't like training or managing? Is there a way for them to be rewarded? What are your experiences relating to the QuikBit content?

Quik BIT 39

Will your new recruit stay?

Ask yourself what you promised. Did you paint pictures as all blue sky so that disappointment was inevitable if things did not always go perfectly?

Right up front, did you explain about the law of averages and why there is no need to feel down or discouraged?

Did you talk about why even a “no” has value?

What about the specific promises you made about what to expect concerning training and your support?

Do you keep close tabs on what happens to new recruits, or do they just become a recruiting success token—a notch on your recruiting belt?

Whether or not recruits stay is a result of your doing what is easy to duplicate, and of showing them exactly how to do it and how to teach others to do it, too.

Just like the three Rs in school, your business has three Rs. In your case the Rs stand for **Recruit** (begin), **Reinforce** (train), and **Retain** (grow together).

Quik BIT 40

What are the first things you did and said?

Training and motivation begin when you first talk to a potential recruit.

Far in advance of the person's decision to be recruited, you have served as a role model.

When the time comes to recruit and motivate others, your initial behavior will be long remembered.

What you said, what you did, what you asked, and what you promised will be recalled.

Your role-modeling will be repeated again and again.

Ask yourself if your approach and your communicating style is good enough to be imitated. Because it will be!

Your recruit's beginning of the beginning is when your influence and responsibility begins.

This is also the source of your recruit's success and, of course, his or her retention.

The way you start determines the finish!

Quik BIT 41

Don't let excitement take over . . .

Signing up a new recruits is a wonderful feeling, but don't let the excitement override the responsibility that you have for their success.

Never let the joy of finding someone with real potential and a strong interest in doing the business blind you to the fact that this person's fate is in your hands.

Your business is easier to do fast than slow. And the speed at which new people get started is almost always an indicator of how far they will go.

Never leave a brand-new recruit without having set realistic goals for the first week and the next few weeks and months. Try to set appointments right away.

Give assignments, have a specific plan for the first week and month, set your next date, and prepare a work schedule that is right for both of you.

Make a genuine commitment to "match their energy."

Do whatever you can to help make sure that the new recruits get their first check in their hands ASAP.

You want it to be like Santa Claus coming early.

Quik BIT 42

People are not sponges . . .

If minds were like sponges or funnels, it would be easy to train people to recruit. But few people "get" all they hear the first time they hear it. Reinforcement is a must!

What you need to teach is the importance of learning from, and duplicating, the actions of successful people in your business. Notice how they listen to the same tapes and lessons over and over? Do you know why?

If you listen to something and take just a few seconds to relate to what you've heard, in those few seconds, you've missed hearing whatever comes next.

You won't get the *full effect of any thought* until you have heard it completely, from beginning to end, several times. *(Research says at least seven times.)*

So make it a habit to reread and to relisten.

There are no dumb questions, and there are no dumb learners, unless it's those who do not listen efficiently and then go on to practice what they think they heard.

The rules: Listen. Practice. Apply. Listen again.

Quik BIT 43

Maintaining recruiting momentum . . .

Because of busy-ness in your life and failing to make a specific time commitment, you may not be maintaining momentum the way you want to.

Maintaining momentum is the secret of successful recruiting. It avoids having to constantly gear up and "re-start" your business.

You can maintain momentum by looking forward. Project your income goal. Compare the time requirements with the time you are willing to invest. Are you being realistic? If needed, add time or reduce goals to take care of unexpected down times.

Plan things to help you stay on the "going somewhere" track. Who can you work with to share what's happening, to talk about QuikBit ideas, and to team up for phone-calling activity?

Ask yourself what might happen to interfere with your goals and schedule. Allow for holidays, family time, and illness. And to maintain your personal momentum, recruit extra people now for the times you won't be able to recruit later.

Reach for a "stretch" goal to help meet your real goal.

Quik BIT 44

There's disappointment and joy . . .

You've often heard nothing is all black or all white, there's always something in between.

Recruiting is like that. Some good stuff, some not so good. What needs to stay good is your attitude!

You find and sign an ambitious newcomer, and it'll never cease to be a joy. If that new recruit doesn't succeed and doesn't stay, it'll be a disappointment.

It is also reality. Frequently, they don't keep on believing they have potential. And belief is everything!

That's why it's critical you always do two things to improve the chances of long-term retention.

One, make certain a new recruit sees success and gets a check as soon as possible.

Two, hang in there. In person, or by phone, be there to help your willing and trainable new recruits over the first hurdles until their feet are firmly planted on the road to success.

Show your joy. It's contagious!

Motivating Yourself

- *Relate recruiting to reality*
- *Consider the joy in sharing*
- *"It's good for you!" doesn't work*
- *We go through life only once*
- *Making extra money is okay*
- *A hangover from childhood*
- *Are you a rescuer?*
- *How are you programmed?*
- *What about treasure hunts?*
- *What does recruiting really mean?*
- *Motivation is simple, IF*
- *The magic of math*
- *Examine your feelings*
- *Get out of your comfort zone*
- *Think of recruiting as a courtship*
- *Passion equals purpose*

Actionators for QuikBits 45–60

QuikBits 45-60 will help you think about some things you will want to consider, explore, change, test, and do to motivate yourself to be a better recruiter and to help others to be recruiters, too.

SELF-EVALUATION

Examine your feelings as you read a particular QuikBit. Were you able to relate to it? If not, do you know why? If so, is this something to think about a little longer and more intensely?

Did you have any hints of either negative or positive feelings as you read the QuikBit? If you did, stop now and zero in on these feelings, trying to analyze what they mean. The hints may be your subconscious saying, "This applies to you. Pay attention!"

ROLE-PLAY

Take turns role-playing a leader talking to someone who just isn't recruiting effectively and is not certain why. Assume that the reason is inherent in the QuikBit you are discussing, and that you want to help the person recognize and deal with it. While role-playing, in your role as a self- or group-trainer, ask questions to pinpoint the problem. Consider what you might say or do to help. Then say or do it, and discuss exactly what you and/or the person will do to take the correct action. The person you are trying to help should respond just as s/he feels the average person would.

Follow each role-player's discussion of what happened and how he or she felt. As the leader, discuss what was good or not so good about each role-playing situation or approach. If you have other ideas related to the situations, be sure to share them.

Quik BIT 45

Relate recruiting to reality . . .

Some people have the mentality that thinks of recruiting in military terms. It's as if they see recruiting as getting ready to go into battle.

In your situation there is no battle. Instead, there is a gift of independence, growth, and a happier and easier future with flexible time.

Recruiting is selecting someone special to whom you want to offer an opportunity to find peace from the pressure of financial insecurity.

You're offering an opportunity to have extra money. To feel a new, growing sense of achievement. To meet new friends and have new goals.

And you're showing people how to be in a position to help themselves and others earn rewards and recognition.

The essence of the word "select" is to choose some *one* from among *many*.

How can that be anything but a very nice, memorable, and meaningful compliment?

Quik BIT 46

Consider the joy in sharing . . .

When you are recruiting, aren't you actually doing a happy thing by sharing happy news?

Think about the tough things people think about, worry about, and get frustrated about.

Imagine all the people who are out there feeling that they don't have any options. Then think about the options you can offer.

If someone were locked away all alone somewhere and could communicate only with you, can you imagine not sharing something good to think about—a chance for change? A chance to be free?

If you could be of help, would you, could you, decide not to share it? Could you walk away when someone really needs you?

If there were a way you could give people an option and some hope, would you deny that to them?

Or would you thank the powers that be that you can share something that will enhance lives and do some good?

Quik BIT 47

"It's good for you!" doesn't work . . .

Imagine children who hate spinach. Then think about the possibility that they hate it because they've heard about other people hating it.

Or maybe they hate it because they have heard so often, "It's good for you!"

Would it have been different if there had been some nice conversation about the delicious flavor or the texture?

Is it possible that because you hear so often in your business that recruiting is "good for you," you end up seeing the task instead of the reward?

Is it possible that you are not motivated by something you're told you have to do, and this blinds you to obvious gain?

The solution is to focus on the benefits—the gain. Doing this may make it easier to get started and to keep going.

Begin to think of recruiting not as "should-eat spinach" but as a really scrumptious dessert.

Quik BIT 48

We go through life only once . . .

In life it is a privilege when we contribute to helping people be happy and successful.

As you reach out to someone when you are recruiting, you are touching and changing lives.

The personal growth, the extra money, the personal and financial rewards of your business touch more than the person you recruit.

The effect of success, achievement, and being happy touches families, friends, and spouses.

It also touches children who learn things about goals that they will probably never learn in school.

It's like you're dropping a pebble and watching ripples spreading outward, expanding the effect of your meaningful action—your recruiting.

Can you just stand on the shore of opportunity, where the view is so lovely, and not even make the effort to reach out to invite someone to share it?

Quik BIT 49

Making extra money is okay . . .

Does making money because of other people's work mentally get in the way of your recruiting?

If you feel guilty, *don't!* The protocol of business everywhere is to reward the leaders.

And if you lead people toward methods of earning money and of finding not only fulfillment but a way to have their efforts recognized, you are entitled to rewards.

Any company is delighted to share earnings with those who help them build their business.

Your recruits know this instinctively. Anything else just wouldn't make sense. Understand this.

And don't focus on the too-generous return on your time investment. Expect and be grateful for it.

Applaud your ability and willingness to help others find what they are looking for—their own business.

Quik BIT 50

A hangover from childhood . . .

Remember when you were a kid, how you felt about the "have-to-do's" the adults demanded.

When it was school time, we wanted to play. When it was playtime, we yearned for school activities and missed doing things with our friends.

When we grew up, too many of us had established a pattern of thinking that "must-do" activities were boring.

And because we hear recruiting is a "must do," maybe we rebel. Or perhaps we find it is difficult to get started with real enthusiasm.

Is recruiting like that for you? Do questions like, "Have you done any recruiting?"and "Did you have any luck?" and "What happened?" bother you?

If recruiting is a chore instead of a personal, rewarding, positive action, isn't it time to act like an adult and do yourself a big favor by recruiting joyously?

Recruiting can mean personal growth, and that can be enriching in a whole lot of ways!

Quik BIT 51

Are you a rescuer?

If there was someone in a deep hole screaming for help, would you reach out and give the person a helping hand?

What if someone in a deep hole lay there whimpering, much too embarrassed to ask for your help? Would your reaction be the same?

Assume you are not endangered, but if you do not offer help, the person may be doomed.

What would you do? If your efforts set the person free, how would you feel?

Naturally, it's possible you could fail and be disappointed and sad—maybe frustrated.

But because you didn't save a particular recruit who really needed activity or cash, would you let that keep you from reaching out to help someone else?

Is there ever any reason to deny help to someone?

And how would you feel if you did?

Quik BIT 52

How are you programmed?

Behavioral scientists and psychologists talk a lot these days about the many ways we mentally program the way we think and feel and act.

What they're talking about is what mothers always have known by instinct.

Remember the little train that said, "I think I can! I think I can!"? That's programming a positive attitude.

When you say that you "aren't having any luck out there recruiting," you are actually programming yourself for poor luck.

When you say, "Everyone's too involved and busy," you are programming yourself to not see the many recruiting opportunities all around you.

What you need is to begin to say, "I will! I will! I will!" And then, almost before you know it, you will, and with great delight, you'll realize that you did!

Your contagious persistence is bound to pay off.

You are capable of programming yourself to make your dreams come true. Why not do it?

Quik BIT 53

What about treasure hunts?

A treasure hunt is a fun party activity where people are given obscure clues to look for things that are usually pretty difficult to find.

Given even the vaguest of clues, persistency usually pays off, because these people search, ask, seek, and try.

And eventually, a surprising number find exactly what they are looking for and end up being winners.

Is the reason you don't recruit enough that you don't have the clues spelled out?

Or do you see the clue, but give up too soon?

Or do you fail to recognize that a clue is often not what it seems, but is only another clue for you to take an entirely different direction?

Is it possible you don't see all the fun and efficiency in using clues to help you recruit?

Or do you lose the spirit of the "game" and quit before you win?

Quik BIT 54

What does recruiting really mean?

What do you think when you hear the word "recruiting"?

Is it something you never seem to have the time to do enough of? Does it remind you of making money, helping others, or winning something? Or is it a drag?

Do you have positive or negative feelings about it? Do you see recruiting as part of your job responsibility, or do you view it as an option? Or a duty?

Is recruiting something you want to do, feel you have to do, or don't like to do?

Have you stopped to examine exactly how you really feel about recruiting?

If you haven't, ask yourself about this, because you really need to understand your feelings.

Could it be that you are afraid to fail? That's okay, just don't run away from the fear. It's natural. Face it!

You call people brave only because they were scared.

The only time you can't afford to fail is the last time you try. So face your fear. It gives you power.

Quik BIT 55

Motivation is simple, IF . . .

To encourage yourself to do anything, you need to have a real "why"—something you want out of YOB—and it needs to be written down as a meaningful objective.

Your "why" should be something you really, really want to accomplish, have, buy, see, or do.

To be meaningful, an objective must be **specific** (with a time frame), **measurable** (with numbers), **realistic** (able to be achieved), and **challenging** (a bit of a stretch). What is your current objective? Is it in writing? And have you shared it with someone?

You don't diet not to eat. You diet to improve your health, or to be a smaller size, or to feel a certain way. You don't want to recruit just to compete or to show off. You want to recruit to grow!

So to motivate yourself, decide what it is you want and what you want to build. Do you want to recruit only because you want to be proud of your business income and how it is growing?

Or, at the same time, wouldn't you feel good when you know that your recruiting is helping others?

Quik BIT 56

The magic of math . . .

Learn how numbers can help you motivate yourself!

Keep score of approaches so you know exactly how many people to talk with to get one recruiting interview.

And how many people on average must hear your story for you to get a "yes"?

Work with and understand your compensation plan so you can put on paper a visualization of how recruiting can add to and multiply your growing income.

Consider recruiting approaches and interview time as *convincing* time, and training time as *building* time.

Like magic, double the value of your time by having local new recruits observe you as you work.

Keep track not only of where you are right now, but also of where you want to be one year or five years from now.

Put numbers and dates in writing, so you can subtract and add as you visualize your needs and progress.

Let the magic of math motivate you!

Quik BIT 57

Examine your feelings . . .

Think about your subconscious, deep-down, hidden-inside feelings about recruiting.

If you are not actively recruiting as a daily part of your work, there have to be some reasons.

To not try to understand that what's happening in your head or your heart is like wearing a blindfold and trying to race up a twisting, steep hill to success.

To understand what motivates or inhibits you is to take off the blindfold so that you can be free to run to the happy place where you were destined to be.

Don't let the race create pressure and stress. If you really believe in you—and in your goal—you won't be stressed. Stress comes from doubts.

Laugh a lot! Secret meetings and no-shows and people who don't do what they say they will are part of the price to pay, and it's well worth it.

So whatever happens, it's happened before. Don't fret. Laugh and go on!

Quik BIT 58

Get out of your comfort zone . . .

Like a little kid dragging around a security blanket, are you dragging around some old fears?

Think of the dragonfly, so ugly as it's growing and so lovely when it breaks out and flies on its own.

If you are limiting yourself to people you know, or who know you, or who you meet in structured situations, you may be cocooning yourself in the temporary security of only the first step to success.

Like the dragonfly, there is a world of "adventure" out there waiting for you to fly out to it.

As you have opportunities to talk to strangers, realize that hearing a compliment from you could not only change their mood, but in some cases, on particular days, it might even change their lives.

If you're too cocooned and shut in being "comfortable," you are denying yourself and others joy!

Can you think of any logical reason to do that?

Quik BIT 59

Think of recruiting as a courtship . . .

Recruiting involves all the elements of a courtship.

It starts with a vision of something we care about and want in life. Isn't that when the steps of personal courtship begin?

The first step is intriguing.
This is the get-acquainted process, where we find out what we have in common, what appeals to us, and whether we want to see more of each other.

Then comes romancing.
This is the convincing process, where we get to know each other better and see if we offer mutual benefits.

The third step is commitment.
This is where the long-term relationship begins.

How long this courtship lasts depends on the recruit's intellectual and emotional involvement and your commitment of support.

The question is whether or not your intentions are honorable.

Quik BIT 60

Passion equals purpose . . .

It isn't enough to work and hope and dream about things you want to do. To be outstandingly successful, you need to have a passion for what you do.

Your passion is what keeps you motivated when things aren't going smoothly.

Your "why" is what motivates you to be in business, but it is your passion that keeps you there and pushes you to move forward to where you want to go.

You need to want something so much that you cannot imagine not doing what needs to be done.

People have a passion for everything, from collecting shoes to playing golf. Only you know your basic passion—which could very well be recruiting.

Passion drives you when you are tired. Passion lifts your spirit when you are down and keeps you hopeful when things go wrong.

Passion is the overriding force behind success.

Passion gives you purpose and helps you plan.

61-63

Using Words That Work

- *Breaking down approach barriers*
- *Presenting your company story*
- *Being prepared for resistance*

Actionators for QuikBits 61–63

Following QuikBits 61, 62, and 63, you will find "Guidelines for Using Words That Work." When using the QuikBits about approaches, refer to the Guidelines that begin on page 120. Do the same thing for presentations and resistance. You can make several training exercises, quizzes, and role plays out of the material in these sections.

DISCUSS the importance of an effective **approach** and **presentation** as well as the importance of being prepared to meet with **resistance**. Review a wide variety of techniques. (If you need help, refer to the ones listed in the Guidelines.) See how many additional ideas you can come up with for specific situations.

ASK for examples of what resistance people have faced during approaches and in recruiting interviews or presentations. (Refer to the Guidelines.) Talk about how they handled it. Explain that being defensive is not a way to win in a communication situation. Resistance is natural, and it is best defeated by empathy and logical clarification.

ROLE-PLAY Define personalities so those involved can pretend to be somebody else. Describe the person and the situation. How did they meet? Where are they? What does the recruiter know about this person? Consider secretly giving the person some specific details about the potential recruit's life or situation that the recruiter will not know so that the "prospect" can prepare appropriate resistance. Use your imagination. Ask them to be natural, but fairly tough in the role-play situations. This is practice that helps get results!

Quik BIT 61

Breaking down approach barriers . . .

Your approach may have to break down the barriers of personal doubts and bad experiences.

Some have tried their own business before and were led astray by false promises, or they may have been psychologically and financially hurt and disappointed.

Good recruiters read books, listen to tapes, and observe and absorb what the successful do and say. They duplicate what works by duplicating the successful.

They learn how the successful handle resistance.

But until you make another's words your own and use them in your "talking" style, they just won't work.

Rehearse an approach script and change words slightly to suit your style. Talk out loud into a mirror until you know you can say what you want without looking at the script. Adapt successful words to fit your style.

Talk out loud until you know that what you say sounds like your own, natural conversational style.

Barriers won't fall if you don't sound like you.

Quik BIT 62

Presenting your company story . . .

When you are ready to give a presentation or interview, it's showtime! The curtain is going up when you are ready to talk about your business.

This is a key moment in recruiting. This is where rehearsal practice pays off. It's where you get applause (a "yes")—or you bore the audience (a "no"), or you get something in between (a "maybe").

This is where your audience decides if you are worth seeing again, because they're interested in what you showed and/or told them or because they like your style.

The price of their ticket is time. Now the decision is whether to invest more time or walk away.

It's not always easy to be on stage. But it's a lot easier when you know you are prepared to do your best because you have invested time and have learned what works from the best.

Preparation helps makes people stars.

Understanding resistance builds relationships.

Good presentations get commitments.

Quik BIT 63

Being prepared for resistance . . .

When you're in the midst of the approach, presentation, or interview, sometimes prospects start nodding their head "yes" almost from the first moment.

If that happens, it's because you made a brilliant approach and "hit a hot button," and those people were all ears and waiting for your message.

That is very nice if it happens, but do not expect it.

More often than not you will face doubts, maybe fears, certainly skepticism, and always, WIIFM. In other words, "What's in it for me?"

If you haven't built WIIFM into what you're saying, you don't deserve a "yes." You'll get a "yes" only by accident.

There's nothing to object to about what you do, or you could not be doing it.

But it is only natural that for self-protection or a desire to know more, you will get some resistance.

Expect resistance. Understand it. And learn what to say when someone resists in any way.

GUIDELINES FOR USING WORDS THAT WORK

Approach Suggestions

What you say and how you say it will determine your success. Here are some proven words and phrases to help you.

We are giving you a wide variety of approach appeals to use in your first contact with potential recruits. We've not covered the many approaches used at in-home Party Plan Shows because this is a key part of Party Plan training programs. However, we know from our workshops that some people in Party Plan never think of appealing to anyone who is not a customer or hostess. They are really missing the boat, because a lot of friends and strangers would like to hear what they do.

Here are approach ideas, but remember, not all will work for all companies.

Curiosity approaches:

- Are you with NOC* yet? (This assumes they will be.)
- Can you imagine what it would be like if you could________?
- Do you know that in only a few hours a week you could______?

Complimentary approaches:

- I have a hunch that you would be terrific doing what I do. So let's have coffee away from here so I can tell you about it.
- Did anyone ever tell you a smile like yours is worth money?
- Watching you, I've a feeling you are just the kind of person I'm looking for. Could we meet and see if you would be even half as excited about my new business as I am?

*NOC stands for Name Of Company; fill in the name of your company.

Imperative approaches:

- ➤ There is something I just have to show you ASAP! Are you free Tuesday or Thursday evening so I could stop by? Or would Saturday morning be better?

- ➤ (*Name*), I need to see you. I've found something, and I have no idea if you'd be interested, but I know you know people I could help. I need your advice. Could we meet either______or_______?

Direct approaches:

- ➤ If I could show you something that makes total sense and could be done in a few hours a week, would you be interested in adding to your monthly income anywhere from $XXX to $XXXX?
- ➤ Assuming you are like most of us, would you like to have a second income if it didn't interfere with what you're already doing? Or how about a new (car, home, travel, etc.)?
- ➤ *If you know the average earnings per hour in your business, as many Party Plan companies do, ask,* How would you like to average $XX an hour, for the hours you choose to work, doing something that will not in any way interfere with your regular job?

Clue-generated approaches:

- ➤ I have an idea that can help you solve that problem. It's something I'm very excited about. We need to talk! How about______?
- ➤ I know several people who were facing the same thing. They found a nifty solution. When can we meet so I can tell you about it?

Research approaches:

- ➤ I'm looking for some people who would like a second income without having to take a second job—who do you know who is worried about money or downsizing, or who is facing sudden extra expenses, or who is interested in building financial security?
- ➤ *Act like a "head hunter."* Is this (*name*)? I understand you are the manager of (*name of store*). Do you have about ninety seconds? This is (*your name*) with NOC, and we're expanding in your area. I understand you know a lot of people, and I'm wondering if you

know anyone who would like an extra $XXX to $XXXX a month without interfering with his or her regular job?

- Do you know anyone who is unhappy with their job yet needs the paycheck, and might like to "job test" while still employed?

Group approaches:

- I'm inviting some of the gang over to hear what I've found that would be fun to do together. And we can make extra money, too. How about being at my place by seven Tuesday evening?
- I've found the most wonderful group of people who are showing me how to have fun making extra money, and I really want my friends to know what I'm doing. We don't see each other enough, so why don't you join us at seven Tuesday night? Trust me. This is really interesting.

Financial approaches:

- Everything is so expensive these days, I wonder if you'd be interested in a way to have extra money?
- *When you get a compliment on something new you are wearing,* say, Thank you. I got it with my NOC check. You've just got to hear about what I'm doing. I am having a ball!

Business approaches:

- I know you're doing very well in your business (or profession), but if there were a generous income opportunity that you could handle alongside your work, would you be interested?
- Are you sick of the rat race yet?
- If my partner and I could show you how, in just a few years, you could have an extra income of XXXX figures, would you take XX minutes to listen to us?
- I'm looking for some new partners who would like to make an extra income alongside what they make now. Want to talk about it?
- I've always respected you as a business person, and now I have discovered something I'd like you to take a look at and give me your opinion on. Have you got about XX minutes?

Time approaches:

- I know how busy you are, so there is something I've just got to show you. What would be the best night this week to meet for coffee?
- Are you going to be home Tuesday night? Good! I'm going to stop by for about XX minutes. I've something to show you.
- Use the "*time-time-why*" approach: I've got one foot out the door *(your time),* but I wanted to call and see if you are going to be home Tuesday or Thursday evening *(their time).* Good! I'm going to run by for XX minutes, I've something to show you *(the "why").* Mention what but *without specific detail.*

Cold call approaches to a salesperson:

- We don't know each other, but I've heard you do a great job as a salesperson for______, and I know we have something in common. We both get much of our business from referrals. I'd like to meet you for coffee—or I'll buy you lunch—to compare notes about how we might help each other. Got your date book handy?
- Every time you go shopping, look for some underpaid but excellent salespeople. There are a lot of them. Shop stores that sell products or services related to what you offer. If you pick a nearby spot for coffee, you can meet with several prospects the same day. Allow plenty of time between appointments and expect some no-shows. Be prepared with something to work on or do in between meetings. Make every moment count.

Cold call approach to a neighbor:

- Hi! This is *(your name)*, your neighbor. Although we haven't talked much, I'd like to have coffee with you. I've discovered something that I think might interest you and some of our neighbors, many of whom you know better than I do. When would be a good time to talk for about XX minutes?

Cold call approach to a young working mother:

- If you are like most of the young mothers I know, you would love to have more quality time with your children. Because I know a way that can happen, I'd like to set up a date to tell you about it. How about meeting for coffee for about XX minutes sometime this week?

Phone call to someone you met briefly:

- Are you interruptible? This is *(your name)*, and I hope you remember me. We met briefly at________, and I've been thinking about you. I'd like to tell you about something that you can do around the edges of your busy life to make a little or a lot of money. You may not remember me, but I remember thinking I ought to talk to you because (etc.).

Phone call to a total stranger:

- Are you free for a couple of minutes? You live in an area where I need ambitious moms—who don't want a full-time job. I can show them how they can increase their income from $XXX to $XXXX a month and have fun doing it. Do you know anyone I should talk to? Someone who likes to help people and would like to earn extra money in a way that suits their life situation?
- I owe you an apology. Have you a minute to talk? This is *(your name).* Someone gave me your name, and I've been carrying it around for a while because I can't remember why I was supposed to call you. By any chance, are you interested in___________? *(Mention things that relate to what you offer.)*

Working a trade show:

- Be subtle, as Show Managers watch for people who are soliciting attendees. When approaching strangers, discuss what they've found interesting. In the process they will tell you a lot about themselves. Then say, "I know something you'd like to know about. Let's exchange cards. We really shouldn't talk about another opportunity here. I'll call you." Pin down a good time to call.
- Or say, "I see you are interested in such and such. There's something I think you might like even better. Would it be okay if I called you at work or at home? Which would be better?"

Working a table:

- ➤ Hopefully you go to meetings, programs, breakfasts, lunches, and dinners that attract the types of people you are looking for. Don't ever monopolize a conversation at your table, but help get people to talk by having everyone tell where they are from or what they do. Collect cards. Keep reminder notes of what you learned to help you when you call them for an appointment.

Network meetings:

- ➤ Prepare for the one-to-two-minute introduction they will allow you. Why not prepare several ideas, so you can alternate what you say at the various meetings?

Getting referrals:

This is one of the very best ways to get excellent new leads to call. People like to be asked for advice, and many people welcome the opportunity to be of help. The fact that you are looking for people who are interested in________ can be a rewarding conversation starter:

- ➤ If you don't get a "yes," at least get a referral
- ➤ If you want to approach people subtly, ask for referrals as your reason for talking to them.
- ➤ If you do business in your neighborhood, you know people who are good with people, such as the local dry cleaner or instant print store owner. Ask who they know who might be interested in ______. Be sure they know that you show people how to_______ so they can recommend that you get together with them to talk.
- ➤ If the product or service you offer represents, or is related to, a certain field (i.e., health, nutrition, beauty, accessorizing, shopping, decorating), talk to people in related services about giving you referrals on a regular basis.

Reminders about appointments:

- ➤ Don't make a "maybe" appointment. If the meeting time cannot be confirmed, make it for another time.
- ➤ Don't see business people in their offices unless they can promise an uninterrupted XX minutes. Always ask about a quiet place near where they work or live.

- Some people are not comfortable inviting you to their home, so suggest alternative places to meet. "We could meet at a quiet restaurant or the lobby of a hotel near where you work or live, or I could come to your home, or you could come to my home office at_______and________. Which is most convenient for you?
- If prospects are too busy to meet, ask if they eat lunch. Then suggest they eat while you talk.
- Never lose sight of your objective in setting a date and time for an appointment. It's simply to create enough curiosity to get a date, but not to tell so much that prospects can decide they are not interested in spending the time to hear more.
- Be excited about seeing them again. Let it show! Doing this is like giving a compliment. They feel they are important.
- Avoid cancellations. Ask, "Can you think of anything that might get in the way of our meeting (*day/time*)?" "Well, let's ink it in our calendar, but if anything does come up, I'd appreciate your calling in advance so I can book this time, okay?"

Presentation Suggestions

Everything you do in your business revolves around the presentation to, or interview of, potential recruits.

Every presentation (or interview) should begin by building on the relationship established when you first approached and intrigued the potential recruit enough that she/he wanted to see you again.

Your objective is to show what your opportunity offers and get a commitment. Remind the potential recruit of why you're there. (The prospect may have forgotten what the appeal was.) Then say, "Mary, you impressed me with your________. Why don't you tell me a bit about yourself?"

The way that you listen, more that anything else, indicates if you just want a new recruit because it'll mean money in your pocket or whether this is someone you like and want to work with and help. And don't overload the prospect. Remember the difference between "need-to-know" and "nice-to-know" information.

It's a good idea to confirm the time required when you begin. Structure what you want to accomplish by saying, "John, in the next XX minutes I want to show you_______. Is that time frame okay with you?" And then go on to cover the four basic elements of every presentation the way you have been trained to do it.

1) **Your story**—why you're doing this and what it has done for you,
2) **The company story**—about image and credibility,
3) **The products or services**—what they will mean to this prospect, and
4) **The compensation program**.

AN IDEA: You can "book-end" your presentation by starting and ending with the reasons people join you. At the end, recap the reasons briefly, and get a commitment by asking, "Which reason seems to fit you best at this time in your life?" An answer is a commitment, so just add, "Well, let me show you how easy it is to get you started."

DO NOT ask things like "Does this interest you?" which can be answered by a "no." Always assume the prospect is going to be, at the very least, a customer or hostess, and at the best—a business builder.

Suggestions for Handling Resistance

Resistance is natural. No one wants to be "sold." People hesitate to make commitments, and there are usually questions they need to ask.

There is not a single "excuse" for a "no" that thousands of others before you haven't heard. So don't get uptight! Know that there are good responses and that training and experience will put the right words on the tip of your tongue. Each company has different things to address, so **listen well to your leaders**. Many of the things you'll hear have been answered in QuikBits. There are some other things to consider, and your leaders know what they are.

One of the most basic responses to a negative answer is called **feel-felt-found**: "I understand how you feel. I felt that way too, but I found . . . ."

Another effective response is **clarification**. "Let me make sure I understand you. Is what you're saying____________?" In doing this, sometimes a clever twist in meaning will cause the prospect to switch direction. If not, be sure to try a powerful question. (Reread QuikBit 22.)

It's also okay to apologize. This gets people off guard and might soften their resistance. Even if you explained something well, say, "I'm sorry, I should have explained more clearly that . . . ."

Be sure to answer questions directly. Never give an answer because you assume you know the reason for the question. When asked a question, you've only got two choices. Answer the question directly, or say you don't know the answer and make a call to get it. Never ignore a prospect's question, although it is all right to ask, "May I answer that later? There's something I want you to know first."

Compliment people for their questions or resistance. It's smart people who tend to examine the pros and cons of things. Ben Franklin did it, and many years later we began to call writing down the pros and cons of something as making a Ben Franklin Sheet. Writing down an expression of thoughts is often a good way to help someone think through a situation and face the challenges and choices.

There are sensible answers to every kind of resistance. When people say they "could never do what you do," know they are either more introverted than you or are shy. Turn that into a benefit. Reassure them. (See QuikBit 32.) If they tell you **they don't have time**, you missed the boat by not talking up front "about wanting to see you because you are so busy."

If they want the security of a regular paycheck, talk about the value of job-testing and that they don't have to leave their job until they can afford it. Or, if you feel **extra money** would be welcome, talk about doing this "alongside their regular job." If you feel they think that working with you would be **in conflict with what they do**, be prepared to explain why it wouldn't.

The "I need to think about it" response is a tough one, so you need to reassure them. How you do that depends on what your program offers. You can certainly try to find out what they are wondering about. Tell them it is a lot easier to think about something when you're with someone who knows about it.

Consider that a desire to "think about it" may be a clue that the person wants to **talk to a spouse** about making a decision. If you think it is, why not say, "Would you like me to meet with you as a couple so you could think about this together?"

A common response is **"I don't know anyone."** New people in an area always feel this way. Reassure them. Say, "I should have mentioned that. I expected you'd feel that way. Many people do. But you know what? That is definitely not something to worry about. I'll show you why when we get together next time." Mention that one of the nicest things about your business that it creates a good way to meet new people.

An easy sort of resistance to deal with is people who feel they **have no skills**. You can make them feel wonderful by showing them they do have "natural skills" that have value. Encourage them to explore this. They'll feel so good when they realize what you said is true.

On the other hand, the most difficult resistance to deal with might be **"I am looking at something else."** Here you need to evaluate their interest in what your company offers and remind them of things that appealed to them when you first talked. Ask for a chance to compare programs. There is probably something about yours that may have more appeal, or benefit them more, or have a competitive advantage over other programs.

Resistance demands preparation. Whatever you do, don't be fatalistic and say to yourself, "Here comes a "no!" Or don't be defensive (taking too strong a stance). The rules are to stay cool, charming, and prepared with logical answers and good common sense. A "no" is not the end of the world. Jim McCune, who believes that "attitude is everything," says to consider getting a "no" as an opportunity to get more practice. As you may well know, the best musicians, the best actors, and the best communicators never stop practicing and improving. Why should you?

Your own resistance is a challenge. If there is any self-sabotage in you, if you keep getting in the way of your success, consider reading *Life Strategies* by Philip McGraw. If you resist working because you need a partner, get one! You can partner by phone if meeting in person is impractical. Learn from your yesterdays and plan great things for your tomorrows. Be sure you don't resist success.

MEMO

From Grandma Sherle and Marlin

We hope this book wasn't fun to read. We hope it made you think and feel and wonder and want to work harder at recruiting better. We hope it challenged you and set you free to grow!

There are no constraints on you. What others have or haven't done has little to do with you. The most important competition you face is with yourself. How does what you do now compare to what you used to do? Are you doing better? Are you doing more? Are you feeling better about your potential? Are you more consistent? More caring?

Do you reach out more? Do you accept responsibility for your success, and do you match energy to help others be successful, too?

Are you going to put this book down and let it gather dust, or do you plan to read it periodically as a reminder? Will you get to know it so well that you can use it as a tool to motivate and to train as well as to help people understand what happens when nothing happens?

We believe in objectives, goals, plans, and action plans. But most of all we believe you should focus on outcomes. What happened? What didn't happen? Why? What can you do differently or better or more often to get the outcome you want?

We hope we've given you ideas and information that make the road to success smoother. You are headed in the right direction, or you would not be reading this book. Good for you!

We have one more question and one more message on the following pages. Please read them and then think about your plans for today.

Be good to yourself! Live up to yourself!

What Happened to Yesterday?

That's the day you were going to do it all, and do it right, and not let yourself be distracted.

It didn't happen. Now, today, you're having a hard time getting started, because you're bogging yourself down with regrets.

The secret of success is to eliminate potential regrets.

Today will be tomorrow's yesterday, so talk to yourself. Plan now to feel good about your accomplishments.

You own a precious gift that no one else can give you—the ability to make a decision about how you spend the tomorrow that will be your yesterday.

Every night ask yourself just two questions: "What did I do today to make someone happy?" and "What did I do today that will in some way specifically affect my objectives?"

Make sure you go to bed with happy answers so you will have no regrets about missed opportunities.

Say "Hello!" to Tomorrow

Today may not have been all that you wanted it to be. Maybe it was your fault! Maybe it was circumstance.

But one thing you can count on is that tonight you can decide what you want tomorrow to be.

Except in rare situations what happens tomorrow is in your hands, and so you have some decisions to make.

What are you going to say "no" to? What are you going to promise yourself? What are your objectives for the day? What are you going to do to prepare for the day?

You'll like yourself better tomorrow night if you plan tonight what to do tomorrow. Then do it tomorrow.

Each day is a special gift to treasure. And each night is the time to remind yourself:

- I am going to be good to me.
- When in doubt, I will reach out.
- I will say "Hello" to each new day, determined to smile and walk in joy!

IDEAS TO CONSIDER WHEN ORDERING

The RECRUITING PROCESS

How are you going to use your books?

- ❒ To sell to people in your organization?
- ❒ To use as a recruiting incentive reward?
- ❒ As part of the cost for attending a special recruiting workshop?
- ❒ For sale after a presentation by an author?
- ❒ For an "autograph & speak" event in a store?
- ❒ As a gift to celebrate a promotion?
- ❒ As holiday or special event personal gifts?

Go to www.GrandmaSherle.com for:

- ➤ Update information on books,
- ➤ Monthly Question & Answer Mailbox,
- ➤ Idea and Leadership Memos, and
- ➤ *Let's Talk About* pages, with ideas to apply to your personal and business lives.

ORDER INFOSTRUCTIONS

The RECRUITING PROCESS

To order copies of *The* **RECRUITING Process,** complete the form below. (*Please feel free to photocopy this form.*)

Consider the Quantity Discounts! Consult the chart below to maximize your savings. These books are wonderful incentives to recruit, or to use as rewards for sales, growth, and promotions.

Book Total: ________ books @ $ ________ per book $__________

Sales Tax: (Alabama Residents add 8%) $__________

Shipping and Handling: (*See chart below.*) $__________

Total Amount Enclosed: $__________

Checks, Money Orders, or Credit Cards accepted. (*No cash please.*)

❒ **Visa** ❒ **Master** ❒ **Discover** Card No.________________ Exp. _____

Ordered By:

Name: (*please print*) ______________________________

Address: ______________________________

City: ________________ State: _____ Zip: ________ Phone: __________

If books are being shipped to a different address, write that address on the back of this form or on a separate piece of paper.

Photocopy this form and mail to:

Grandma Sherle, Inc., 16061 Carmel Bay Road, Northport, Alabama 35475
Phone: (205) 330-5661, Fax: (205) 330-1705

Orders will also be accepted at: www.GrandmaSherle.com
or via e-mail at: Orders@GrandmaSherle.com

Book Pricing

Quantity	Price Per Book	S&H Per Order
1	$14.95	$2.95
2-5	$14.50	$4.00
6-10	$14.00	$7.50
11-25	$13.75	$10.00
26-50	$13.45	$17.50
51-100	$13.25	$25.00

SPECIAL DISCOUNT SAVINGS

Buy a case of 54 books for only $700.00

INCLUDING
Shipping and Handling